Samantha

Samantha

A Soap Opera and Vocabulary Book for
Students of English as a Second Language

Meryl Robin Becker

Ann Arbor
THE UNIVERSITY OF MICHIGAN PRESS

Copyright © by the University of Michigan 1993
All rights reserved
ISBN 0-472-08178-0
Library of Congress Catalog Card No. 95-63234
Published in the United States of America by
The University of Michigan Press
Manufactured in the United States of America

2005   2004   9   8   7

To the students and staff at Employment Connections, Inc.,
and Adult Basic Education in Chelsea, Massachusetts,
and to my family, Rachel, Sarah, and Rick

Contents

Chapter **1**

Bradley Is Troubled

Chapter *1*

Bradley Is Troubled

Part 1

Vocabulary

These are the vocabulary words you will learn in this chapter. Each word has a definition and a sentence. Notice that many words have more than one meaning.

1. **intelligent** (adjective) — smart
   He had an intelligent idea.

2. **magnificent** (adjective) — beautiful, great
   He went to see the magnificent mountains of New Hampshire.

3. **butcher** (noun) — a person who kills animals for food and cuts up and sells the meat; (verb) — to kill animals for food
   The butcher weighed the steaks.
   The farmer is going to butcher his biggest pig for Christmas dinner.

4. **through**
   1) (preposition) — from one side of something to the other
      Read through the whole sentence before you write in the answer.
   2) (preposition) — because of
      She got the apartment through a friend.
   3) (preposition) — in, between, among
      I had to go through all the shoes to find the one I liked.
   4) (adjective) — finished
      She's through cleaning now.

5. **concentrate**
   1) (noun)—something with the water taken out to make it stronger, thicker; **concentrated** (adjective)—stronger, thicker
      You add water to orange juice concentrate.
      This shampoo is concentrated.
   2) (verb)—to keep your thoughts on one thing
      She tried to concentrate on the teacher's words.
   3) (verb)—to bring together in one place
      All the stores are concentrated in the downtown area.

6. **enough** (adjective); (adverb)—as much as is needed
   Is there enough soup?
   Is the soup hot enough?

7. **medical** (adjective)—having to do with making sick people well
   He went to medical school to become a doctor.

8. **secretary** (noun)
   1) a person who works in an office typing, putting things in alphabetical order, or answering the phone
      The secretary was typing a letter.
   2) a person who is the head of a department of the government
      The secretary of defense gives advice to the president when there is a war.

9. **troubled** (verb)
   1) worried
      He was troubled when his daughter didn't call.
   2) in pain
      She is troubled with a sore back.

10. **sigh**
    1) (noun)—a deep breath let out because of being sad or tired; (verb) to let out a deep breath.
       The sad woman gave a big sigh.
       He sighed when I gave him the bad news.
    2) (verb)—to make a sound like a sigh
       The old couch sighed when she sat on it.

11. **rather** (adverb)
    1) prefer, want (used with *would*)
       I would rather have chocolate than vanilla.
    2) more correctly speaking
       Look the word up in that book, or rather, that dictionary.
    3) more than a little
       She came to school rather late.

12. **excitement** (noun)—high interest, strong feelings
    Everyone noticed his excitement when the movie star came to town.

Idioms

Idioms are words that have special meanings in English when used together.

1. **if only**—a wish that something were not true
   If only I hadn't lost the money.

2. **look up to**—to see a person as better than you, to admire
   The little boy looked up to his father.

3. **after all**—giving a reason or example
   Of course he's tired. After all, he worked all day.

4. **want out of**—to want to leave or not do something
   He wanted out of the agreement.

5. **break someone's heart**—to hurt someone's feelings or disappoint someone very much
   If I don't visit my mother on her birthday, it will break her heart.

Part 2

Vocabulary

Complete each of the following sentences with one of the vocabulary words on the list. Don't forget to read the words before the blank *and* the words after the blank to help you find the missing vocabulary word.

Remember that all of the answers (a, b, c) under one number are different meanings of the same word. When a word has more than one meaning, there is a parenthesis ( ) after the sentence. In the parenthesis put the number of the meaning from the vocabulary list in Part 1. For example, in number 4 of the following exercise:

4. (a) I tried to _____ on the instructions so that I would know what to do. ( )

Look back at the vocabulary list in Part 1, number 5, "concentrate." Which meaning does this sentence use, meaning 1), 2), or 3)? Number 2) means to keep your thoughts on one thing, and that is something you need to do to read instructions, so you would put a 2 in the parenthesis.

4. (a) I tried to <u>concentrate</u> on the instructions so that I would know what to do. (2)

enough	butcher
magnificent	concentrate
secretary	sigh
intelligent	through
rather	troubled
medical	excitement

1. I asked the _____ to cut the chicken into small pieces.

2. He's not stupid; he's very _____ .

3. The _____ church was one of the most beautiful I'd ever seen.

4. (a) I tried to _____ on the instructions so that I would know what to do. ( )

   (b) _____ (d) apple juice is cheaper than fresh apple juice. ( )

   (c) All the dirt is _____ (d) in the corners of the room. ( )

5. (a) The _____ was typing and answering the phone. ( )

(b) The president of the United States appoints the _____ of education. ( )

6. (a) She looks _____ because of all the problems she has on her mind. ( )

(b) He is _____ by frequent headaches. ( )

7. Two doctors and four nurses work at the _____ center.

8. (a) I'd _____ go to a concert than to the movies because I love music. ( )

(b) I'm feeling _____ sleepy. ( )

(c) We left at 2 A.M. Saturday night, or _____ , Sunday morning. ( )

9. (a) The trees _____ (ed) in the wind. ( )

(b) She was so tired that she gave a big _____ when she sat down. ( )

10. (a) He walked _____ the park to the hotel on the other side. ( )

(b) She looked _____ the papers to find the one she wanted. ( )

(c) He became rich _____ hard work. ( )

(d) I'm _____ with work at 5:00. ( )

11. There is _____ food for everybody.

12. There was a lot of _____ in the family when she won the money.

Idioms

Complete each of the following sentences with one of the idioms on the list. Don't forget to read the words before the blank *and* the words after the blank to help you find the missing idioms.

if only   after all
look up to   wanted out of
                    break her heart

1. He hated his boss so he _____ his job.

2. _____ I had called first. I would have found

   out that the store was closed.

3. They _____ the famous movie star.

4. If he tells her that he doesn't love her, it will _____

   _____ .

5. I'm leaving now. _____ , it's late.

Part 3

Questions to think and talk about before you read:

- In the country you come from, what is important in a marriage? Should marriage be exciting and fun?
- What are some of the reasons a husband and wife would want to leave each other?

Episode 1. Bradley Is Troubled

Bradley was troubled. He couldn't concentrate on his work. All he could think of was Gloria, Gloria—her face, her hair, her eyes! He sighed. If only he was married to her rather than to Samantha. Samantha and he had been married too long. After three years, there was no excitement left. Anyway, a man wants a woman who will look up to him. Samantha was too intelligent for him. After all, she was a medical secretary and worked in an office. He was a butcher and worked with his hands. Gloria was a magnificent looking woman, and that was enough for him. He was through with Samantha. He would tell her so, tomorrow. No, he'd call her now!

He picked up the phone and put it down again. Samantha was still his wife. He just couldn't tell her he wanted out of the marriage. It would break her heart.

Part 4

Questions

1. How is Bradley feeling? Why?
2. Who does Bradley love?
3. Who is Bradley married to?
4. What is he thinking about doing?
5. Do you agree with Bradley that three years is too long to be married? Why or why not?
6. Do you agree with Bradley that a man wants a woman who will look up to him? Should a man be smarter than his wife or girlfriend? Why or why not?
7. Is a person who works in an office always more intelligent than a person who works with his hands?
8. Does Bradley decide to leave Samantha? Why or why not?

Part 5

Fill in the blanks with your vocabulary words (use one word twice).

1. prefer   _____

2. person who cuts meat   _____

3. wonderful   _____

4. pay attention   _____

5. smart   _____

6. finished   _____

7. sound of sadness   _____

8. something about a hospital   _____

9. worried   _____

10. going in one side and coming out the other _____

11. person who works in an office   _____

12. strong feelings   _____

13. as much as needed   _____

Part 6

There are nine vocabulary words spelled incorrectly in this copy of the story. Find the mistakes and correct them. The first one has been done for you.

          troubled
    Bradley was ~~trobled~~. He couldn't consentrat on his work. All he could think of was Gloria, Gloria—her face, her hair, her eyes! He siged. If only he was married to her rater than to Samantha. Samantha and he had been married too long. After three years, there was no excitement left. Anyway, a man wants a woman who will look up to him. Samantha was too intelijent for him. After all, she was a medical secratery and worked in an office. He was a bucher and worked with his hands. Gloria was a macnifecent looking woman, and that was enough for him. He was threw with Samantha. He would tell her so, tomorrow. No, he'd call her now!

    He picked up the phone and put it down again. Samantha was still his wife. He just couldn't tell her he wanted out of the marriage. It would break her heart.

Chapter 2

Samantha Notices Something Strange

Chapter 2

Samantha Notices Something Strange

Part 1

Vocabulary

These are the vocabulary words you will learn in this chapter. Each word has a definition and a sentence. Notice that many words have more than one meaning.

1. **poor** (adjective)
   1) having very little money
      The poor woman didn't have enough money for food.
   2) feeling sorry for
      Bradley wants to leave poor Samantha.
   3) bad
      He's in poor health.
      The sweater was of such poor quality that I had to return it to the store.

2. **pour** (verb)
   1) to move liquid from one place to another
      He poured the water from the bottle into the glass.
   2) to have a lot of something moving from one place to another
      The people poured into the movie theater.
   3) to rain heavily
      Take your umbrella. It's pouring.

3. **perfume** (noun) — good-smelling liquid worn by women
   Judy put on some perfume before she went to the party.

4. **prominent** (adjective)
   1) important, famous
      Everyone came to see the prominent movie actor.
   2) large, sticking out
      The tall Christmas tree was prominent in the room.

5. **recently** (adverb)—happening a short time ago
   My sister had a birthday recently.

6. **strange** (adjective)
   1) not usual or normal
      He is a strange person who does strange things.
   2) not known
      Nobody knew the strange man on the beach.

7. **ridiculous** (adjective)—silly, funny
   *Painting one wall pink and the other wall purple would look
      ridiculous.*

8. **country**
   1) (noun)—land not in a town or city, often farmland
      Faith lives on a farm in the country.
   2) (noun)—a nation, area with one government
      Vietnam is the name of a country.
   3) (adjective)—a kind of American music most popular in the west-
      ern part of the United States and in country areas; also called
      cowboy music
      Mary likes country western music.

9. **brought** (verb)—past tense of *bring;* to carry something to someone
   I brought a cake to the party.

10. **bought** (verb)—past tense of *buy;* to get by paying money
    They bought tickets for the movie.

11. **involve** (verb)
    1) to pay complete attention to something
       *She was so involved in watching the movie that she didn't hear
          the phone ring.*

2) to be a part of, to be connected to
   She is involved in a political party.
3) to be connected by love; to be boyfriend and girlfriend
   Paula and Milt are becoming involved.
4) has in it, contains
   Cleaning dishes involves washing, rinsing, and drying them.

12. **tremble** (verb)
    1) to shake
       When the wind blows the leaves tremble.
    2) to shake from fear, anger, cold, or excitement
       He was trembling from the cold.

Idioms

Idioms are words that have special meanings in English when used together.

1. **as soon as** — quickly, at the same time as
   We will eat as soon as Mary comes home.

2. **a lot** — a large amount, much
   He eats a lot.

3. **oh my goodness** — an expression showing some surprise
   Oh my goodness, it's raining!

Part 2

Vocabulary

Complete each of the following sentences with one of the vocabulary words on the list. Don't forget to read the words before the blank *and* the words after the blank to help you find the missing vocabulary word.

Remember that all of the answers (a, b, c) under one number are different meanings of the same word. When a word has more than one meaning, there is a parenthesis ( ) after the sentence. In the parenthesis put the number of the meaning from the vocabulary list in Part 1. For example, in number 1 of the following exercise:

1. (a) She is a _____ lawyer; everyone has heard of her. ( )

Look back at the vocabulary list in Part 1, number 4, "prominent." Which meaning does the sentence use, meaning 1) or 2)? Number 1) means important, famous, and the sentence says everyone has heard of her, so you would put a 1 in the parenthesis.

1. (a) She is a <u>prominent</u> lawyer; everyone has heard of her. (1)

ridiculous	strange
recently	perfume
poor	pour
tremble	country
prominent	brought
involve	bought

1. a) She is a _____ lawyer; everyone has heard of her. ( )

   b) In the movie *Roxanne*, the man has a large, _____

   nose. ( )

2. Sarah's new _____ smells very nice.

3. a) The house would _____ every time a train passed by. ( )

   b) When the man pointed the gun at her, she started to

   _____. ( )

4. The last time I saw Mary was three months ago. I haven't seen her

   _____.

5. a) It's raining so hard that it's _____ (ing). ( )

   b) Please _____ the juice into the glass. ( )

   c) When he put an ad in the newspaper, the answers

   _____ (ed) in. ( )

6. With his silly clothes and his big shoes the clown looked

 _____ .

7. a) This _____ is called the United States. ( )

   b) He doesn't live in the city. He lives in the _____ . ( )

   c) Kenny Rogers is a _____ western singer. ( )

8. Today I didn't bring my pencil, but yesterday I _____ it.

9. After I got paid yesterday I _____ some new clothes.

10. a) He's never been here before, so our town is _____ to

   him. ( )

   b) Seeing a ghost is a _____ experience. ( )

11. a) People who have no money are _____ . ( )

   b) The screwdriver was of such _____ quality that it broke

   the first time I used it. ( )

   c) The _____ little girl has no parents. ( )

12. a) Going to school _____ (s) hard work. ( )

   b) He was _____ (d) in a plan to rob the bank. ( )

   c) She didn't hear me because she was completely _____ (d)

   in her work. ( )

   d) He's _____ (d) with a beautiful woman. ( )

Idioms

Complete each of the following sentences with one of the idioms on the
list. Don't forget to read the words before the blank *and* the words after
the blank to help you find the missing idioms.

   as soon as
   oh my goodness
   a lot

1. A million dollars is _____ of money.

2. The family will move into the apartment _____

   the painters finish painting the living room.

3. _____ , I forgot to get the laundry!

Part 3

Summary

Bradley is thinking about leaving his wife Samantha for his girlfriend Gloria.

Questions to think and talk about before you read:

- What are some signs that might tell Samantha that Bradley loves someone else?
- How do you think Samantha will feel if she finds out Bradley loves Gloria?

Episode 2. Samantha Notices Something Strange

Samantha thought about her husband Bradley. "He's been doing strange things recently," she thought. "When we went out to the country on our vacation he was on the phone a lot. He works late hours and comes home smelling of perfume." Samantha decided to talk to him about it as soon as he came home.

"Bradley," she said, "I think you are involved with another woman." Bradley started to laugh. "That's ridiculous," he said, but when he tried to pour himself a cup of coffee his hands started to tremble. He brought the cup to his lips but he couldn't drink it.

"It's true!" he said suddenly. "Gloria is the most wonderful woman in the world! I love her!"

"Gloria!" said Samantha. "Do you mean Gloria, the prominent country music singer?"

"That's right," said Bradley. "She bought a big house in Nashville and I'm going to live there with her."

"Oh my goodness," thought Samantha, remembering her years living with Bradley. "Poor Gloria."

Part 4

Questions

1. What are two of the reasons why Samantha thinks that Bradley is seeing another woman?
2. What does she decide to do about it?
3. Why are Bradley's hands trembling? Why couldn't he drink his coffee?
4. What is Gloria's job?
5. What does Bradley want to do?
6. What does Samantha mean by "poor Gloria"? What does this tell us about how she feels about Bradley?
7. In the last part of this story Bradley was afraid to leave Samantha because he thought it would break her heart. Do you think his leaving will break her heart? Why or why not?

Part 5

Complete this crossword puzzle with words from your vocabulary list.

Down

1. If you have no money you are _____.
5. Something you're connected to you're _____ (d) in.
6. The opposite of the city is the _____.
7. The past of bring is _____.
9. Something you've never seen before is _____.
10. A well-known person is _____.

Across

2. When you put milk in a cup you _____ it.
3. Something silly is _____.
4. A short time ago is _____.

7. The past of buy is _____ .
8. A sweet-smelling liquid is _____ .
11. When you shake all over you _____ .

Part 6

There are ten vocabulary words spelled incorrectly in this copy of the story, and one word has been spelled wrong two times. Find the mistakes and correct them. The first one has been done for you.

     Samantha thought about her husband Bradley. "He's been doing
strange
~~stranje~~ things resently," she thought. "When we went out to the contry

on our vacation he was on the phone a lot. He works late hours and

comes home smelling of perfume." Samantha decided to talk to him

about it as soon as he came home.

     "Bradley," she said, "I think you are involved with another

woman." Bradley started to laugh. "That's rediculous," he said, but when

he tried to pore himself a cup of coffee his hands started to trembel. He

broght the cup to his lips but he couldn't drink it.

     "It's true!" he said suddenly. "Gloria is the most wonderful woman

in the world! I love her!"

     "Gloria!" said Samantha. "Do you mean Gloria, the prominant

countri music singer?"

     "That's right," said Bradley. "She bougt a big house in Nashville

and I'm going to live there with her."

     "Oh my goodness," thought Samantha, remembering her years living with Bradley. "Poor Gloria."

Chapter 3

Getting Stuck at the Bank

Chapter 3

Getting Stuck at the Bank

Part 1

Vocabulary

These are the vocabulary words you will learn in this chapter. Each word has a definition and a sentence. Notice that many words have more than one meaning.

1. **stick** (past tense—*stuck*) [see Idioms #1]
   1) (verb)—to put on or be attached, as with glue
   The boy tried to stick the paper on the wall with tape.
   The car was stuck in the mud.
   2) (verb)—to force someone to do or accept something she doesn't like
   They always stick him with the worst job.
   When her roommate suddenly moved out, she got stuck paying the whole month's rent herself.
   3) (verb)—to push out of, extend
   If your sweater sticks out of the suitcase, you won't be able to close it.
   4) (verb)—to touch with something sharp and make a hole in it
   Stick the knife into the cake and cut the first piece.
   5) (noun)—a thin piece of wood
   Annie put some sticks on the fire.

2. **hear** (verb)
   1) to get sound into the ears
   I hear music.
   2) to get news or information
   Did you hear anything from your brother in California?

3. **here** (adverb)—in this place
   Here is your notebook.

4. **gasp** (verb)
   1) to take in air quickly, usually in surprise or fear
      He gasped when the robber took out a gun.
      "It's true! I won a million dollars!" Nanette gasped.
   2) to have difficulty taking in air
      The people on the beach heard the boy gasp for air as he went under the water.

5. **throat** (noun)—the front part or inside of the neck
   When he caught a cold, his throat hurt.

6. **account**
   1) (noun)—amount of money put in or taken out of the bank
      Rachel has almost $200 in her checking account.
   2) (noun)—story, explanation
      The policeman wrote down the woman's account of how the accident happened.
   3) take into account (idiom)—to pay attention to, consider
      She packed a lot of sweaters into her suitcase because she was trying to take the cold weather into account.

7. **balance**
   1) (noun)—what is left, especially with money
      After he wrote a check for the new chair, his checking account balance was only $10.00.
      Take half of the medicine today, and the balance tomorrow.
   2) (verb)—to keep steady or even; to make one thing the same as another; (noun) steadiness or evenness; sameness between two things
      To balance your checkbook, what you take out must equal what you put in.
      He tried to balance ten plates on one hand.
      It's hard to keep your balance when standing on one foot.
      Robin tried to have a balance between the needs of her children and the needs of her job.

8. **teller** (noun)—a person working in a bank who takes in and gives out money
    I gave the teller my $200 paycheck and he gave me $200 in cash.

9. **deposit**
    1) (verb)—to put money into the bank; (noun)—money put into the bank
       On payday they deposit their checks into the bank.
       This check is a deposit for my account.
    2) (noun)—part of the price paid to show you want to buy something and will pay the rest later
       If you give me a $100 deposit now, you can pay the rest off at $20 a month.

10. **withdraw** (verb)
    1) to take away
       Juan had to withdraw his name from the contest because his brother was president of the company.
    2) to take money out of the bank
       Please withdraw $20 from my account.

11. **joint**
    1) (adjective)—done or shared by two or more people, together
       The two brothers are joint owners of the car.
    2) (noun)—the place where two parts, especially bones, come together
       Your finger has two joints.

12. **sneaky** (adjective)—secret in a way that is not fair or honest
    When nobody was looking, the sneaky man tried to get into the movie without paying.

Idioms

Idioms are words that have special meanings in English when used together.

1. **the words seemed to stick in her throat**—she had trouble speaking, out of fear or surprise [see Vocabulary #1]

   "Who's there?" she asked, but when she saw the man hiding behind the door, the words seemed to stick in her throat.

2. **get away with**—do something wrong without anyone stopping or punishing you

   You can't get away with anything when Mother is watching!

3. **get a hold of yourself**—control your feelings

   You must stop crying now. Get a hold of yourself.

Part 2

Vocabulary

Complete each of the following sentences with one of the vocabulary words on the list. Don't forget to read the words before the blank *and* the words after the blank to help you find the missing vocabulary word.

Remember that all of the answers (a, b, c) under one number are different meanings of the same word. When a word has more than one meaning, there is a parenthesis ( ) after the sentence. In the parenthesis put the number of the meaning from the vocabulary list in Part 1.

deposit	sneaky
gasp	balance
throat	here
stick	hear
joint	account
withdraw	teller

1. Please come over _____ where I am.

2. a) He gave me an _____ of what happened. ( )

   b) I have a savings _____ at the bank. ( )

c) He ran out of food because he forgot to take his sister's friends into _____ . ( )

3. a) Speak louder; I didn't _____ what you said. ( )

   b) Did you _____ about the movie? ( )

4. a) He licked the stamp to make it _____ to the paper. ( )

   b) I saw the little girl _____ her tongue out at her brother. ( )

   c) Then the brother hit his sister with a wooden _____ . ( )

   d) The child tried to _____ the balloon with a pin. ( )

   e) She tried to _____ me with doing the dishes. ( )

5. a) After running the five-mile race he started to _____ . ( )

   b) The pain was so bad that he gave a loud _____ . ( )

6. Fran gave the _____ $10 to deposit into her account.

7. He coughed when he got some food stuck in his _____ .

8. a) An elbow or a knee is a _____ . ( )

   b) We made a _____ effort to get the door open. ( )

9. a) He needed money, so he had to _____ $100 from his savings account. ( )

   b) Next week the army will _____ its troops from the city. ( )

10. a) When he got paid he made a $50 _____ into his checking account. ( )

   b) She put a $100 _____ on the furniture she was buying. ( )

11. a) He lost his _____ and fell off his bike. ( )

   b) What is the _____ in my checking account? ( )

12. I can't trust that man. He's too _____ .

Idioms

Complete each of the following sentences with one of the idioms on the list. Don't forget to read the words before the blank *and* the words after the blank to help you find the missing idioms.

> get away with
> get a hold of
> words seemed to stick in her throat

1. Robbers steal because they think they can _____
   it.
2. After the accident, the frightened driver tried to _____
   _____ himself.
3. She started to ask, "Is Grandfather better?" but when she saw
   Grandmother crying, the _____ .

Part 3

Summary

Bradley tells Samantha that he is leaving her for Gloria, a country western singer.

Questions to think and talk about before you read:

- Who gets the money, furniture, and other belongings when married people leave each other?
- Do you think Bradley and Samantha will be fair to each other?

Episode 3. Getting Stuck at the Bank

"Well!" thought Samantha, "Bradley thinks he can leave me and do whatever he wants. He's probably planning on taking everything with him, but he won't get away with it. I'm not getting stuck!" She waited until she could hear Bradley leave the house. Then she drove to the bank where she and Bradley had their joint savings account.

She walked up to the teller and told her that she wanted to withdraw all of the money in the account. Then she heard a voice behind her. "Making a deposit, my dear?"

"Bradley!" gasped Samantha. The words seemed to stick in her throat. "What are you doing here?"

"The same thing you are, I think. Before you withdraw anything, why don't you ask what the balance is?"

The teller looked at her sadly. "$3.73," she said.

Samantha began to tremble. She tried to get a hold of herself. All the money was gone! She hadn't taken into account that Bradley was sneaky, sneakier than she was. Of all the women in the world, she was the stupidest!

Part 4

Questions

1. Where does Samantha go?
2. What does she mean by, "I'm not getting stuck"? What does she plan to do?
3. What kind of bank account do she and Bradley have?
4. Who does she see at the bank?
5. What is the account balance?
6. What did Bradley do?
7. How does Samantha feel at the end?
8. Was Bradley fair to Samantha? Was Samantha fair to Bradley?

Part 5

Fill in the blanks with words from the vocabulary list. On the left are the letters of the word you need, but the letters are not in the correct order.

1. itskc   A little piece of wood is a _____.

2. agsp   When you're surprised you _____.

3. lltere   Person who takes your money in a bank. _____

4. roahtt   Where your food goes to get to your stomach.

    _____

5. hrea   Something you do with your ears. _____

6. ccoanut   Something you open in the bank. _____

7. rhiwtdwa   Taking money out of the bank. _____

8. opdesit   Putting money into the bank. _____

9. rehe   Where you are is right _____.

10. labnaec   When you slip on the ice in wintertime, you lose your

    _____.

11. iojnt   Together _____

12. asenyk   Something in secret _____

Part 6

There are nine vocabulary words spelled incorrectly in this copy of the story, and one word has been spelled wrong two times. Find the mistakes and correct them. The first one has been done for you.

"Well!" thought Samantha, "Bradley thinks he can leave me and do whatever he wants. He's probably planning on taking everything with him, but he won't get away with it. I'm not getting stuck!" She waited until she could ~~here~~ hear Bradley leave the house. Then she drove to the bank where she and Bradley had their joint savings acount.

She walked up to the teller and told her that she wanted to

witdraw all of the money in the account. Then she heard a voice behind her. "Making a diposet, my dear?"

"Bradley!" gasped Samantha. The words seemed to stik in her throat. "What are you doing hear?"

"The same thing you are, I think. Before you withdraw anything, why don't you ask what the balanse is?"

The teler looked at her sadly. "$3.73," she said.

Samantha began to tremble. She tried to get a hold of herself. All the money was gone! She hadn't taken into accont that Bradley was sneaky, sneakier than she was. Of all the women in the world, she was the stupidest!

Chapter 4

A Walk on the Beach

37

Chapter **4**

A Walk on the Beach

Part 1

Vocabulary

These are the vocabulary words you will learn in this chapter. Each word has a definition and a sentence. Notice that many words have more than one meaning.

1. **handsome** (adjective)
   1) good-looking, usually in a man
      The women turned around to look at the handsome man.
   2) large, generous
      Thank you so much for the handsome gift.

2. **decision** (noun)—a choice of what to do, conclusion
   A decision was made to close the school because of snow.
   The judge made a decision on the court case.

3. **amateur**
   1) (noun)—someone who plays a sport or uses a talent for fun, not for pay; (adjective)—done by someone who plays a sport or uses a talent for fun, not for pay
      The actors in our high school play are amateurs, but I think they're very good.
      Only amateur runners, not paid professionals, can play in the Olympics.

2) (noun)—beginner, person with little experience; (adjective)—done by a beginner or person with little experience

Compared to an experienced gardener like you, I am just an amateur.

My daughter Sarah is an amateur cook, so sometimes she needs help.

4. **instead** (adverb)—in place of another

Star Market is closed, so let's go to Stop & Shop instead.

5. **continue** (verb)—to go on, keep going

The weather will continue to be rainy until next week.

6. **beat** (verb)
   1) to repeat a sound, as in a heart or drum

   Elizabeth beat her hands to the sound of the music.
   2) to win over

   Sam's team beat our team in baseball.
   3) to hit

   Two big boys beat him on his way home from school.
   4) to mix strongly

   Lillian beat the cake with an egg beater.

7. **appointment** (noun)
   1) time planned to see someone

   I have an appointment to see my son's teacher.
   2) naming someone to a certain job

   The governor's appointment of a new judge to the State Supreme Court was in all the newspapers.

8. **champagne** (noun)—a white wine with carbonation, or bubbles, in it

Charlie drank champagne at the party.

9. **wonder**
   1) (noun)—something great or surprising, or causing such a feeling

   Steve is learning about the wonders of modern medicine.
   2) (verb)—to think about and want to know or understand

   I wonder where Jack is tonight.

10. **familiar** (adjective) — well known, seen before
    "Silent Night" is a familiar Christmas song.
    She got lost because she is not familiar with our town.

11. **depressed** (adjective) — very sad; (verb) — to make sad
    The depressed man tried to kill himself.
    Being sick so long depressed me.

12. **against** (preposition)
    1) touching
       She put the bookcase against the wall.
       We could hear the rain beating against the window.
    2) on the other side of, not agreeing with
       "No," Kenny's mother said, "I'm against your playing football.
       It's too dangerous."
       The Red Sox are playing against the Yankees.

Idioms

Idioms are words that have special meanings in English when used together.

1. **looking into her eyes** — looking at someone in a loving way
   Pam and Michael ate dinner by candlelight, looking into each other's
   eyes.

2. **catch himself** — stop himself
   He tried to catch himself before he said something he'd be sorry for.

3. **what the heck** — showing that you're not worried or you don't care
   about what happens
   The dress was too much money, but Pat loved it. "What the heck,"
   she said, "I'll take it."

4. **who needs it?** — showing you don't need or want someone or some-
   thing. This is a question that does not need an answer.
   This car is always giving me trouble. Who needs it? I'll take the bus.
   He's against everything I do. Who needs him?

5. **I'd love to**—I would like very much to do whatever was asked. This is a short answer to a question. (I'd is the contraction for *I would*.) *"Would you like to go to a party?" "I'd love to." (The long answer would be, "I'd love to go to a party" or "I would love to go to a party.")*

Part 2

Vocabulary

Complete each of the following sentences with one of the words on the list. Don't forget to read the words before the blank *and* the words after the blank to help you find the missing vocabulary word.

Remember that all the answers (a, b, c) under one number are different meanings of the same word. When a word has more than one meaning, there is a parenthesis ( ) after the sentence. In the parenthesis put the number of the meaning from the vocabulary list in Part 1.

depressed	continue
familiar	amateur
against	champagne
beat	decision
wonder	instead
appointment	handsome

1. a) Sometimes I _____ about the meaning of life. ( )

   b) This new computer is really a _____. ( )

2. a) We read about the _____ of the president's secretary of state. ( )

   b) I have an _____ to see the doctor at 3 P.M. ( )

3. a) Paul Newman, the movie star, is a _____ man. ( )

   b) They are offering a _____ reward for the person who finds their lost dog. ( )

4. Marta felt _____ after her mother died.

5. I've seen you somewhere before. You look _____.

6. I've made a _____. I'm going back to school.

7. a) He doesn't get paid to play college football. He's an _____ player. ( )

   b) I don't know much about sewing; I'm just an _____. ( )

8. a) I'm not in favor of the new law. I'm _____ it. ( )

   b) Sit up straight with your back _____ the back of the chair. ( )

9. She started to stop at the first gas station, but then she decided to _____ on to the next one.

10. The store didn't have apple juice so I got orange juice _____.

11. At special times, like New Year's and weddings, people drink _____.

12. a) He _____ his hands against the door, but no one heard. ( )

    b) Judy _____ the eggs before putting them in the pan. ( )

    c) I heard his heart _____ when I put my ear to his chest. ( )

    d) The Red Sox had more points, so they _____ the Yankees. ( )

Idioms

Complete each of the following sentences with one of the idioms on the list. Don't forget to read the words before the blank *and* the words after the blank to help you find the missing idioms.

catch himself   looking into her eyes
what the heck   who needs her
I'd love to

1. Before he could _____ , he saw that he'd eaten

   half of the cake.

2. "I love you," Romeo said to Juliet, _____ .

3. I'm on a diet, but _____ , pass me the ice

   cream.

4. If she won't help me, I'll do it myself. _____ ?

5. Would you like to dance? _____ .

Part 3

Summary

Bradley is leaving his wife Samantha for Gloria. When Samantha goes to the bank to withdraw money, she finds out Bradley has already withdrawn it all.

Questions to think and talk about before you read:

- What do you think Samantha will do now?
- Where do you go when you're feeling sad or depressed?

Episode 4. A Walk on the Beach

Samantha drove home from the bank feeling depressed. "I wonder what I should do now?" she thought. "Everything is going against me." Suddenly she stopped the car. "Why should I go home?" she thought, and she went to the beach instead.

Walking on the beach always made her feel better. "Who needs Bradley anyway?" she thought. Just then she looked up and saw a familiar face. It was John Paul, the handsome young doctor from the hospital where she worked.

"Samantha!" smiled John Paul, taking her hands. "How glad I am to see you!"

"Why?" she said, before she could catch herself.

"Ah," he said, looking into her eyes, "because it is so sad to walk on the beach alone, don't you agree?"

"Uh, yes," she said, her heart beating faster.

"Yes, the beach!" he continued, taking her hand and walking with her. "We all need a little vacation from our regular lives. No appointments! No problems! Would you like a glass of champagne?"

He handed her a glass and took a small bottle of champagne from the box under his arm.

"But," she said, "You have two glasses. How did you know I . . . ?"

"I knew," he said, holding her hand tighter. "Why don't we walk the beach all afternoon together?"

She thought for a minute and then made a decision. She was an amateur at this kind of thing, but what the heck. "I'd love to," she said, smiling.

Part 4

Questions

1. How is Samantha feeling when she leaves the bank? Where does she go?
2. Who does she see there?
3. What does he say and do when he sees her?
4. How is Samantha feeling? What words tell you how she is feeling?
5. What does he give her to drink?
6. Why do you think he is carrying this bottle and two glasses with him on the beach?
7. What does he ask her to do? Do you think it's okay for her to say yes?
8. What does Samantha mean by, "She was an amateur at this kind of thing"?

Part 5

Can you guess these riddles? Fill in the blanks with your vocabulary words.

1. When you don't know what you want to do, you can't make a

    _____ .

2. Beautiful looks in a man. _____

3. When you hit something over and over again. _____

4. How something looks when you've seen it before. _____

5. Something you drink when you say, "Happy New Year!"

    _____

6. What you do when you go on and on and on and don't stop.

    _____

7. In place of another. _____

8. Something you do when you think and think and try to understand.

    _____

9. How you feel when life is sad and terrible. _____

10. If you don't agree with it you're _____ it.

11. When you agree to meet someone you make an _____ .

12. Something a Yankee baseball player or a Celtics basketball player

    is *not.* _____

Part 6

There are nine vocabulary words spelled incorrectly in this copy of the story. Find the mistakes and correct them. The first one has been done for you.

                                                    depressed
    Samantha drove home from the bank feeling ~~depresed~~. "I wunder

what I should do now?" she thought. "Everything is going agenst me." Suddenly she stopped the car. "Why should I go home?" she thought, and she went to the beach insted.

Walking on the beach always made her feel better. "Who needs Bradley anyway?" she thought. Just then she looked up and saw a familiar face. It was John Paul, the hansome young doctor from the hospital where she worked.

"Samantha!" smiled John Paul, taking her hands. "How glad I am to see you!"

"Why?" she asked, before she could catch herself.

"Ah," he said, looking into her eyes, "because it is so sad to walk on the beach alone, don't you agree?"

"Uh, yes," she said, her heart beating faster.

"Yes, the beach!" he continued, taking her hand and walking with her. "We all need a little vacation from our regular lives. No apointments! No problems! Would you like a glass of shampane?"

He handed her a glass and took a small bottle of champagne from the box under his arm.

"But," she said, "You have two glasses. How did you know I . . . ?"

"I knew," he said, holding her hand tighter. "Why don't we walk the beach all afternoon together?"

She thought for a minute and then made a dicision. She was an amature at this kind of thing, but what the heck. "I'd love to," she said, smiling.

Chapter 5

A Fight

Chapter 5

A Fight

Part 1

Vocabulary

These are the vocabulary words you will learn in this chapter. Each word has a definition and a sentence. Notice that many words have more than one meaning.

1. **enormous** (adjective)—very large; very many
   The elephant is an enormous animal.
   There is an enormous number of people in the world.

2. **stair, stairs** (noun)—step; a number of steps, one after the other
   He stopped on the first stair and put his coat on.
   These stairs go up to the second floor.

3. **stare** (verb)—to look at steadily for a long time, usually out of surprise or great interest
   Everyone turned to stare at the magnificent hat the queen was wearing.
   She just stares at anyone who speaks to her because she doesn't understand English.

4. **wave**
   1) (verb)—to move a hand to say hello or goodbye; (noun)—movement of a hand to say hello or goodbye
      Wave bye-bye to Papa.
      She gave a wave to her husband from the window.
   2) (verb)—to move from side to side
      The wind made the flag wave.

3) (noun)—a round shape or curve of water that goes up and down
   An enormous wave came over her as she stood in the ocean, and she almost fell.
4) (noun)—a round shape or curl of hair; (verb)—to make such a shape
   Her long hair fell in waves down her back.
   Her hair was straight, so she waved it with a curling iron.
5) (noun)—the sudden movement of a strong feeling or condition
   We had a cold wave when the weather stayed at 5°F for a week.
   Gary looked at his baby and felt a wave of love.

5. **employee** (noun)—person paid to work for a person or a company
   This company has 100 employees.

6. **employer** (noun)—a person or company who pays workers to work
   The United States government is the largest employer in the country.

7. **bother**
   1) (verb)—to give trouble to, upset; (noun)—trouble, worry
      Loud noises bother me.
      I'm sorry to bother you, but can you tell me how to find the post office?
      It's too much of a bother to cook in hot weather.
   2) (verb)—to take the trouble
      Don't bother to pick me up at school. I can take the bus.

8. **wealthy** (adjective)—rich
   The prominent senator was also wealthy and handsome.

9. **dismiss** (verb)
   1) to not allow to keep a job
      Noé dismissed the plumber because he did such a poor job.
   2) to send away, allow to leave
      The teacher said, "I will dismiss the class as soon as everyone has finished."
   3) to stop thinking about
      I decided the plan was too sneaky, so I dismissed it from my mind.

4) to decide not to charge someone under the law
   There was excitement in the courtroom when the judge decided to dismiss the charges brought against the secretary.

10. **polish** (verb)—to make shiny; (noun)—cream or wax used to make things shine; shininess
    George polished the car until it shone like a mirror.
    Shoe polish will make your shoes look much better.
    The table has a beautiful polish to it.

11. **by** (preposition) (notice the difference in spelling: *bye*—goodbye, and *buy*—to get by paying for) [see Idioms #1].
    1) before, not later than
       Please deposit this check by tomorrow.
    2) near
       I saw you when I passed by in my car.
       Put the lamp by the big chair.
    3) shows who did something
       "Hamlet" is a play by Shakespeare.
    4) shows in what way
       Janel came by train.

12. **outfit** (noun)
    1) clothes that go together
       Jill bought a new outfit for the party; the pants, blouse, and shoes look nice together.
    2) a group that works together, especially soldiers
       One of the soldiers in his outfit was hurt.

Idioms

Idioms are words that have special meanings in English when used together.

1. **come by**—come [see Vocabulary #11]
   We came by last night but you weren't home.

2. **try on** — to put on to see if it fits or if you like it
   I need to try on this shirt to see how the color looks on me.
   Before you buy clothes you should try them on.

3. **how sweet** — very nice or loving (in the same way that sweet is something with sugar in it that tastes nice, a person who is sweet is nice or loving)
   How sweet your baby is.

4. **sweetie** — a loving name for someone you care about, someone who is nice (*dear* has the same meaning)
   Where are you going, sweetie?
   You're a real sweetie to help me this way.

5. **life savings** — money a person has saved over many years or over a whole life; all the money a person has
   When Marta got sick, she used up her life savings to pay the hospital bill.

Part 2

Vocabulary

Complete each of the following sentences with one of the words on the list. Don't forget to read the words before the blank *and* the words after the blank to help you find the missing vocabulary word.

Remember that all the answers (a, b, c) under one number are different meanings of the same word. When a word has more than one meaning, there is a parenthesis ( ) after the sentence. In the parenthesis put the number of the meaning from the vocabulary list in Part 1.

wealthy	dismiss
wave	stare
bother	stair
employee	enormous
employer	outfit
polish	by

1. I've never seen such a big house; it's _____ .

2. a) Children! Please don't _____ me when I'm on the

    phone! ( )

   b) Don't _____ to get up. I can get it myself. ( )

3. The _____ woman gave $100,000 to our school.

4. a) I came to school _____ bus. ( )

   b) This book is _____ a famous writer. ( )

   c) She likes to keep her baby close _____ . ( )

   d) Please be at school _____ 9:00. ( )

5. The old lady had such a funny hat on that I started to _____

    at her.

6. Be careful when you walk up the steps; one _____ is

    broken.

7. a) The little girl began to _____ goodbye to her grand-

    mother. ( )

   b) During a storm there are a lot of _____ (s) in the

    ocean. ( )

   c) We had a heat _____ of 90° weather for a month. ( )

   d) The wind made the branches of the tree _____ back and

    forth. ( )

   e) Her curly hair has beautiful _____ (s) in it. ( )

8. a) This skirt and sweater will make a beautiful _____. ( )

   b) When he was in the army his _____ won an award. ( )

9. She is an _____ of Boston City Hospital — she works there.

10. My _____ said she would give me a raise when I had

   worked there for six months.

11. a) It was so hot that the teacher decided to _____ the

   class. ( )

   b) AIDS is such a dangerous disease that we cannot _____

   its importance. ( )

   c) When the judge found out the witness was lying, he

   _____(ed) the charges against the defendant. ( )

   d) The bank decided to _____ the teller when he couldn't

   balance the money he took in or gave out. ( )

12. Iris used silver _____ to shine her silver plate.

Idioms

Complete each of the following sentences with one of the idioms on the list. Don't forget to read the words before the blank *and* the words after the blank to help you find the missing idioms.

sweetie	how sweet
come by	try on
	life savings

1. Can you _____ my house at 4:00?

2. _____ these shoes to see if they fit.

3. _____ of you to send me flowers.

4. I like to call my daughter _____.

5. She used her _____ to buy a house.

Part 3

Summary

Bradley is leaving Samantha for Gloria. After finding out Bradley has taken all the money out of their joint checking account, Samantha meets John Paul on the beach.

Questions to think and talk about before you read:

- What are some of the things you remember about Gloria? What does she look like? What is her job?
- What kind of person do you think Gloria is?

Episode 5. A Fight

After leaving the bank, Bradley drove over to Gloria's house. Gloria lived in an enormous house in the wealthy part of town. Bradley found her busy trying on country western outfits in her purple and pink bedroom. The room was full of her employees and clerks from all the best stores.

"Oh, hi sweetie," said Gloria as she tried on a pink cowboy hat. "How nice of you to come by. How do you like this hat?"

"Gloria," said Bradley, standing behind three women handing cowboy boots to their employer. "Guess what? I got all the money out of my joint checking account at the bank!"

"Oh Bradley," said Gloria, waving her hand as a woman put nail polish on it. "Why did you bother? Let the poor little thing have it. I have plenty of money."

"But I did it for you," called Bradley loudly because he could not get near her.

"How sweet," answered Gloria as she picked up the phone. "We can use the money to go out sometime, or use it to buy yourself a new outfit. See you later, dear."

"What!" yelled Bradley. "Buy a new outfit with it? This is my life savings!"

Gloria put down the phone and she and everyone else in the room turned around to stare at Bradley.

"You stand around trying on clothes and dismissing me and my whole life! Is this what I left Samantha for?!" And with that Bradley ran down the stairs and out of the house.

Part 4

Questions

1. What does Gloria's house look like? Where is it?
2. What is Gloria doing?
3. Who else is in the room with her?
4. Is Gloria happy that Bradley has taken the money out of his bank account? Why or why not?
5. Who is she talking about when she says, "Let the poor little thing have it?"
6. Name two different things Gloria is doing while Bradley is talking to her.
7. What does Gloria say Bradley should do with the money?
8. Why does that make Bradley angry?
9. Does Gloria want Bradley to stay or has she dismissed him? How do you know?
10. Why does everyone stare at Bradley?
11. Do you agree that Bradley has a right to be angry?

Part 5

Can you guess these riddles? Fill in the blanks with your vocabulary words.

1. What you do with your hand when you say goodbye. _____

2. You need them to go from the basement to the roof. _____(s)

3. What you are when you have a lot of money. _____

4. Something bigger than big. _____

5. A person who works for someone else. _____

6. The someone else in number 5.   _____

7. This book is _____ a famous writer.   _____

8. What you put on your shoes to make them shiny.   _____

9. What people do when you wear your ridiculous
   green and purple t-shirt with the matching hat
   and shoes.   _____

10. What you are wearing in number 9.   _____

11. When you think what someone says is not impor-
    tant or not true, you _____ it.   _____

12. What a fly does to you when he's buzzing around
    your head.   _____

Part 6

There are nine vocabulary words spelled incorrectly in this copy of the story. Find the mistakes and correct them. The first one has been done for you.

After leaving the bank, Bradley drove over to Gloria's house.
Gloria lived in an ~~enormos~~ ^{enormous} house in the welthy part of town. Bradley

found her busy trying on country western outfits in her purple and

pink bedroom. The room was full of her employes and clerks from all

the best stores.

"Oh, hi sweetie," said Gloria as she tried on a pink cowboy hat.

"How nice of you to come buy. How do you like this hat?"

"Gloria," said Bradley, standing behind three women handing

cowboy boots to their employer. "Guess what? I got all the money out

of my joint checking account at the bank!"

"Oh Bradley," said Gloria, waving her hand as a woman put nail palish on it. "Why did you bothr? Let the poor little thing have it. I have plenty of money."

"But I did it for you," called Bradley loudly because he could not get near her.

"How sweet," answered Gloria as she picked up the phone. "We can use the money to go out sometime, or use it to buy yourself a new outfit. See you later, dear."

"What!" yelled Bradley. "Buy a new outfit with it? This is my life savings!"

Gloria put down the phone and she and everyone else in the room turned around to stair at Bradley.

"You stand around trying on clothes and dismising me and my whole life! Is this what I left Samantha for?!" And with that Bradley ran down the stares and out of the house.

What Is a Soap Opera?

Part 1

Questions to think and talk about before you read:

- Do you know what a soap opera is?

In the last five *chapters* you have been reading a continuing story about Samantha, Bradley, and Gloria. This kind of story is called a "soap opera" in English. Many of you have seen or read stories like this in your countries. There are many soap operas, or "novelas," in Spanish, for example. But what is an American soap opera, and what does "soap" have to do with it?

Soap operas are continuing stories. They are divided into parts, or *episodes*, that continue from day to day or from week to week. Most of them are shown on television during the day, usually in the afternoon. The people in them are troubled by many problems. None of them seems to be very poor, and many of them are wealthy, but they all have lives full of love and hate and constant change. The stories are about the happiness of being in love, of people getting married and people leaving each other, of sickness, sex, drugs, death, and almost any other problem you can think of. Their lives are never simple. They have some of the same problems we all have, just many more of them. In fact, it would be almost impossible for real people to have so many interesting and unusual problems.

People like to watch soap operas because many of the stories are about love and *romance.* People like to watch them because the *characters*, or people in the stories, have exciting lives. Soap operas are also exciting to watch because each *episode*, or *chapter*, stops in the middle of the story, and we are left wondering what will happen. Will Bradley leave Samantha? Will Samantha keep seeing John Paul? Most important of all is that people like you and me like soap operas because we feel involved with the *characters* in the stories. We hate the bad *characters* and we get angry at them. We feel sad for the *characters* we like who are depressed, and feel happy when things go well for them. Sometimes the stories go too far. They have things in them that would probably not happen to a real person. The *characters* get too excited and too emotional. But if the stories and the *characters* involve us in their lives, we keep watching or keep reading.

Why are they called "soap operas?" When these kinds of stories were first shown on radio and TV, the program would stop, and someone would come on selling soap for washing floors or clothes or dishes. These *advertisements*, or *commercials*, paid for the programs. Because there were so many *advertisements* for soap, the programs began to be called soap operas. The word "opera" comes from an Italian word for a dramatic and emotional musical story. Soap operas today have *commercials* for other things besides soap, but they are still called soap operas.

Part 2

Questions

1. Are soap operas shown in one part or many parts?
2. When are they usually on television?
3. Name three kinds of problems you see on soap operas.
4. Name two reasons that people like to watch soap operas.
5. What are some of the ways people feel when they get involved in watching a soap opera?
6. Why is the word "soap" in soap operas?
7. Have you ever watched soap operas on television? What do you think of them?
8. Are there differences between American soap operas and soap operas in your country?

Part 3

Vocabulary

There are a few new words in what you have just read. You should be able to understand the meanings of these words by reading the words *before* and *after* them. Usually the definition of the word is in the same sentence as the word.

Fill in the blanks with the words that go with the definitions. If there are two blanks next to a definition, it is because there are two words with the *same* definition. If you're not sure of the meanings of the words look back at the story.

episode	character
chapter	commercial
advertisement	romance

1. love story   _____

2. person in a story   _____

3. part of a story   _____

                                       _____

4. notice that tries to sell something   _____

                                       _____

Part 4

Vocabulary Review

This is a review of all the vocabulary words you have learned in Chapters 1-5. Match each word on the left with the correct definition on the right by putting the correct letter in the blank. Look back at the words in the chapters if you need help with any of the definitions.

Chapters 1-3

A.

1. concentrate	_____	a. to glue
2. strange	_____	b. past of buy
3. stick	_____	c. having to do with making sickness better

4.	enough	_____	d.	worried
5.	country	_____	e.	think on one thing
6.	medical	_____	f.	where there are farms
7.	ridiculous	_____	g.	past of bring
8.	hear	_____	h.	silly
9.	here	_____	i.	not usual, different
10.	brought	_____	j.	in this place
11.	bought	_____	k.	what is needed
12.	secretary	_____	l.	use your ears
13.	sigh	_____	m.	person who works in an office
14.	tremble	_____	n.	a sound of sadness
15.	troubled	_____	o.	shake

B.

1.	gasp	_____	a.	place in your neck
2.	intelligent	_____	b.	something that smells good
3.	excitement	_____	c.	finished
4.	prominent	_____	d.	a short time ago
5.	throat	_____	e.	a sound of surprise
6.	magnificent	_____	f.	to rain a lot
7.	poor	_____	g.	person who cuts meat
8.	pour	_____	h.	smart
9.	account	_____	i.	to be part of, connected to
10.	perfume	_____	j.	strong feelings
11.	recently	_____	k.	prefer
12.	butcher	_____	l.	famous
13.	rather	_____	m.	great
14.	involve	_____	n.	not good, not well done
15.	through	_____	o.	story, explanation

Chapters 3-5

A.

1. bother	_____	a. money left in the bank
2. wealthy	_____	b. step
3. instead	_____	c. hit
4. balance	_____	d. good-looking
5. stare	_____	e. person who works in a bank
6. stair	_____	f. keep going
7. beat	_____	g. move a hand to say goodbye
8. teller	_____	h. to upset
9. against	_____	i. done in secret
10. continue	_____	j. rich
11. wave	_____	k. beginner
12. handsome	_____	l. look at
13. sneaky	_____	m. choice
14. amateur	_____	n. in place of another
15. decision	_____	o. not agreeing with

B.

1. champagne	_____	a. worker for someone else
2. dismiss	_____	b. to think about
3. employee	_____	c. clothes that go together
4. employer	_____	d. someone who has people work for her
5. familiar	_____	e. time to meet
6. deposit	_____	f. near
7. wonder	_____	g. send away
8. withdraw	_____	h. done together
9. polish	_____	i. bubbling wine
10. appointment	_____	j. to make shiny
11. joint	_____	k. known
12. depressed	_____	l. very big
13. outfit	_____	m. to put money in the bank

14. by _____   n. sad
15. enormous _____   o. to take money out of
                             the bank

Part 5

Idioms Review

This is a review of all the idioms you have learned in Chapters 1-5.
Match the part of the sentence on the left that goes together with the
end of the sentence on the right by putting the correct letter in the
blank.

Chapters 1-3

1. If . . .   _____   a) break my
2. I don't like this place.   heart.
   I want . . .   _____   b) all, it's
3. She tried to hide the   lunchtime.
   money but she won't   c) my goodness!
   get . . .   _____   d) seemed to
4. Ten pages of home   stick in her
   work is a . . .   _____   throat.
5. A present for me!   e) out of here.
   Oh . . .   _____   f) up to her
6. She was so surprised   mother.
   that when she tried to   g) only I had a
   talk, the words . . .   _____   big car.
7. Let's eat. After . . .   _____   h) a hold of
8. We can leave as . . .   _____   himself.
9. If I lose my favorite   i) soon as I put
   ring it will . . .   _____   on my coat.
10. The little girl   j) away with it.
    looks . . .   _____

11. When he saw his
    hands were trembling
    he tried to get . . .   _____

Chapters 4–5

1. I'm tired, but what
   the . . .   _____
2. Try . . .   _____
3. There was so much
   ice in the street that
   before she could
   catch . . .   _____
4. I can drive you home
   if I come . . .   _____
5. This book is really
   bad, who . . .   _____
6. My mother calls
   me . . .   _____
7. Would I like to have
   some more cake? I'd
   love . . .   _____
8. "Will you marry me?"
   he asked, looking
   down . . .   _____
9. How . . .   _____
10. The money in the
    bank is my life . . .   _____

k) lot to do.

a) needs it?
b) sweet of you to
   give flowers.
c) to.
d) savings.
e) into her eyes.
f) on this hat.
g) heck, let's go
   out.
h) herself she fell.
i) by the school
   this afternoon.
j) sweetie.

Chapter 6

A Surprise at the Beach

Chapter 6

A Surprise at the Beach

Part 1

Vocabulary

These are the vocabulary words you will learn in this chapter. Each word has a definition and a sentence. Notice that many words have more than one meaning.

1. **funny** (adjective)
   1) something that makes you laugh
      Joe told a funny joke and we all laughed.
   2) strange
      There was a funny smell in the room.

2. **expect** (verb)—to wait for something, thinking it will probably happen
   I expect it to be a cold winter.
   She is expecting a baby in July.

3. **waist** (noun)—the middle part of the body between the chest and the stomach
   In this dance the man puts his hands around the woman's waist.

4. **waste**
   1) (verb)—to make poor use of something, to use more than is needed; (noun)—poor use of something
      I hate to waste time standing in line.
      This radio was a waste of money; it's already broken.
   2) (noun)—garbage, things to be thrown away
      After Tahlia finished cutting out her drawing, she threw the waste in the wastepaper basket.

5. **mad** (adjective)
   1) angry
      Rachel gets mad if the other children touch her things.
   2) crazy
      The man who killed all those people must have been mad.
   3) liking very much, crazy about
      Robin is mad about her husband.

6. **furious** (adjective)
   1) very angry
      When Dan saw the milk all over the floor, he was furious at the children.
   2) wild, violent
      The furious storm scared Tobey.

7. **selfish** (adjective) — a person who thinks only of himself and not of other people
   He's so selfish. He drank all the champagne and didn't leave any for me.

8. **drop**
   1) (verb) — to fall or let fall; (noun) — a sudden fall or decrease in something
      Nina dropped the books on the bed.
      I'm so tired I feel like I'm going to drop.
      Tonight there will be a drop in temperature.
   2) (verb) — stop, leave out, let go
      I don't like to hear about things like that. Please drop it and talk about something else instead.
      To change "cry" to "cried" drop the "y" and add "ied."
      She used to be his girlfriend but he dropped her.
   3) (noun) — a small amount of water or other liquid in a round shape
      Give baby Mike one drop of this medicine three times a day.
      I felt a drop of rain.
   4) drop out (verb) — to leave or stop attending
      She dropped out of the class when her son got sick.

9. **bent**—past tense of *bend*
   1) (verb)—to curve over, to fold; (adjective)—curved over, folded; curved, crooked
      Superman bent the metal rod.
      This knife is bent.
   2) (verb)—to curve the body over
      She bent over to pick up the pencil she dropped.

10. **lean**
    1) (verb)—to bend to the front or side or back
       She leaned out of the window to call her daughter in for dinner.
    2) (verb)—to rest one thing against another to help hold it up
       Josefa leaned her bicycle against the fence.
    3) (verb)—to turn to for help
       After his wife died, Tuy leaned on his mother for help with the children.
    4) (adjective)—without fat, thin
       Lean meat is less greasy than meat with fat on it.
       Jimmy Stewart is tall and lean.
       He remembered the lean years when they had very little to eat.

11. **froze** (verb)—past tense of *freeze*
    1) to change water or other liquid to ice
       The water in the glass froze when she left it outside.
    2) to feel very cold
       His mother said he would freeze if he went out without a coat and it was true, he froze.
    3) to stop moving or stand very still out of fear or surprise, as if frozen
       "Freeze!" yelled the police, and the robber froze with her hands in the air.

12. **soft** (adjective)
    1) not hard to the touch; easy, not hard (not difficult)
       Santos sat on the soft bed.
       These tomatoes are soft; don't buy them.
       He's so wealthy that he lives a soft life.

2) quiet, nice, nice to touch
   A soft light was shining on her soft hair.
   He talked softly as soft music played.

3) gentle, kind
   Her eyes were soft as she looked at her child.

4) weak
   Working at a desk would make me soft if I didn't swim every night.
   Don't be soft. Tell him the truth even if it hurts.

5) without alcohol
   Coke and orange soda are soft drinks.

Idioms

Idioms are words that have special meanings in English when used together.

1. **pay attention to** — listen to, watch, notice
   Johnny, pay attention to the teacher.
   The man doesn't pay enough attention to his son.

2. **fix things up** — to make things better
   There are clothes all over the room and papers on the floor. We need to fix things up in here.
   I had a fight with my wife, but tonight I'm going to bring her flowers and fix things up with her.

3. **turn around** — to turn or move to the opposite direction
   He turned around to see what was behind him.

4. **at least** — a minimum; the basic, most important thing
   I have no more money, but at least there is food in the house.

5. **so mad he didn't know which way to go first** — when a person is so angry that he doesn't know what to do or where to go
   After the fight with her mother, Louise was so mad she didn't know which way to go first.

Part 2

Vocabulary

Complete each of the following sentences with one of the words on the list. Don't forget to read the words before the blank *and* the words after the blank to help you find the missing vocabulary word.

Remember that all the answers (a, b, c) under one number are different meanings of the same word. When a word has more than one meaning there is a parenthesis ( ) after the sentence. In the parenthesis put the number of the meaning from the vocabulary list in Part 1.

waist	waste
soft	bent
froze	lean
drop	expect
furious	mad
selfish	funny

1. a) When he found out his car had been stolen he was

   _____ . ( )

   b) The _____ growth of the grass was caused by all the

   rain. ( )

2. a) She has 200 records; she's _____ about music. ( )

   b) When Vinny and Rebecca had a fight, they were both

   _____ . ( )

   c) The _____ woman did a lot of strange things. ( )

3. The _____ boy took all the candy for himself.

4. a) You're carrying too many plates. Be careful you don't

   _____ them. ( )

   b) When his father died, he had to _____ out of school and

   get a job. ( )

c) When I found out that his account of the accident was a lie, I

_____ (ped) his story from the accident report. ( )

d) Put one _____ of vanilla in the cake. ( )

5. a) This was the first time I'd been to Denver, but it looked famil-

iar. I had a _____ feeling I'd been there before. ( )

b) I like _____ movies because they make me laugh. ( )

6. a) The river was dirty and polluted because the _____

from the factory went into the water. ( )

b) If you take more food than you can eat, you _____

food. ( )

7. You wear a belt around your _____ .

8. a) I _____ when I went out in the snow, so I went home to

warm up. ( )

b) When the weather got cold last week, the lake _____ . ( )

c) The woman _____ when she saw the car coming at her,

and her son had to pull her out of the way. ( )

9. a) I can't use this nail; it's _____ . ( )

b) She _____ over to pick up her son. ( )

10. a) The man with the broken leg _____ (ed) on a cane. ( )

b) He _____ (s) on his friends when he needs help. ( )

c) David _____ (ed) forward to see the game better. ( )

d) _____ meat is better for you than meat with a lot of fat

on it. ( )

11. a) Juice and Pepsi are _____ drinks. ( )

b) He has become _____ because he doesn't exercise. ( )

c) _____ music helps me to go to sleep. ( )

d) She cried when she saw the sad movie because she has a

_____ heart. ( )

e) The pillow is _____ . ( )

12. I _____ him to be here any minute.

Idioms

Complete each of the following sentences with one of the idioms on the list. Don't forget to read the words before the blank *and* the words after the blank to help you find the missing idioms.

> fix things up
> pay attention
> turn around
> at least
> so mad he didn't know which way to go first

1. Some things in the house are broken, and it needs paint, but when I

_____ in there it will look beautiful.

2. You'll get lost if you don't _____ to the directions I'm giving you.

3. I forgot to give Hannah her hat, but _____ she has a warm coat.

4. We're lost. Let's _____ and go back.

5. When he found out his car had been stolen, he was

_____ .

Part 3

Summary

Bradley is leaving Samantha for Gloria. Bradley takes all the money out of their joint checking account, Samantha meets John Paul on the beach, and Bradley gets angry at Gloria.

Questions to think and talk about before you read:

- What do you think Bradley will do now?
- Who do you think Bradley really loves, Gloria or Samantha?

Episode 6. A Surprise at the Beach

When Bradley left Gloria's house he was furious. He stood outside for a minute because he was so mad he didn't know which way to go first. "Why did I ever leave Samantha?" he thought. "That Gloria is so selfish. When I go to see a woman I expect her to drop whatever she's doing to be with me. I'll go find Samantha and see if I can fix things up with her. At least she pays attention to me."

He drove home, but Samantha wasn't there. "I know!" he thought. "When she wants to think she goes for a walk on the beach."

When Bradley got to the beach he ran out onto the sand. He didn't want to waste any time finding Samantha. He looked around and then he saw her. "That's funny," he thought. "I wonder who that is with her." As he got closer, he suddenly froze. A man was standing near her with his hands around her waist. As he watched, the man bent down and kissed her.

Bradley turned around quickly and ran back to the car. He leaned against the car and closed his eyes. When he opened them he saw Gloria standing in front of him.

"I couldn't let you leave like that," she said softly.

Part 4

Questions

1. How is Bradley feeling about Gloria when he leaves her house?
2. How is he feeling about Samantha? Why?
3. Bradley says, "When I go to see a woman I expect her to drop whatever she's doing to be with me." Do you agree that a woman should drop everything for a man? Should a man drop everything for a woman?
4. Why does Bradley think Samantha will be at the beach?

5. What does he see on the beach that makes him suddenly freeze?
6. How does he feel when he leans against the car and closes his eyes? Why do you think he feels that way?
7. Who does he see when he opens his eyes?
8. What does she say?
9. What do you think will happen now?

Part 5

Fill in the blanks with words from the vocabulary list. On the left are the letters of the word you need, but the letters are not in the correct order.

1. dam   When you're angry, you're _____.

2. oufrisu   When you're very, very, *very* angry, you're _____.

3. ufnny   Something that seems strange. _____

4. sifeslh   When you keep all the candy for yourself and won't give anybody any, you're being _____.

5. pord   Another word for letting something fall. _____

6. tosf   Something that's not loud. _____

7. pxeect   When your friend says he'll help you, you _____ him to do it.

8. awste   When you throw things away that you could have used better. _____

9. tawis   The place that has a button on your jeans. _____

10. erfoz   Something you put in the freezer *yesterday*. _____

11. nebt   When your car has an accident, the fender gets

           _____.

12. aeln   When you're not strong enough you _____ on another person for help.

Part 6

There are eight vocabulary words spelled incorrectly in this copy of the story. Find the mistakes and correct them. The first one has been done for you.

When Bradley left Gloria's house he was ~~furius~~ furious. He stood outside for a minute because he was so mad he didn't know which way to go first. "Why did I ever leave Samantha?" he thought. "That Gloria is so selfish. When I go to see a woman I expec her to drap whatever she's doing to be with me. I'll go find Samantha and see if I can fix things up with her. At least she pays attention to me."

He drove home, but Samantha wasn't there. "I know!" he thought. "When she wants to think she goes for a walk on the beach."

When Bradley got to the beach he ran out onto the sand. He didn't want to waist any time finding Samantha. He looked around and then he saw her. "That's funy," he thought. "I wonder who that is with her." As he got closer, he suddenly frose. A man was standing near her with his hands around her waste. As he watched, the man bent down and kissed her.

Bradley turned around quickly and ran back to the car. He leened against the car and closed his eyes. When he opened them he saw Gloria standing in front of him.

"I couldn't let you leave like that," she said softly.

Chapter 7

Should a Man Come First?

Chapter 7

Should a Man Come First?

Part 1

Vocabulary

These are the vocabulary words you will learn in this chapter. Each word has a definition and a sentence. Notice that many words have more than one meaning.

1. **possible** (adjective)—able to happen [see Idioms #2]
   It's not possible for me to get here by 8:00.

2. **pale** (adjective)
   1) white or light in color [see Idioms #3]
      Her skin was pale because she never went out in the sun.
   2) a color that is not dark
      This paint you bought is rather pale. I think we need something darker.

3. **pail** (noun)—a round container for holding or carrying water or other things; bucket
   The little boy poured sand into his little red pail.

4. **shovel** (noun)—a wide piece of metal or plastic with a holder used for picking things up; (verb)—to use a shovel or something that looks like one
   We need a big shovel to shovel away all this snow.
   The little girl used a cup to shovel the sand into the pail.

5. **reply** (verb)—to answer; (noun)—an answer
   I asked Gary directions to the school and he replied with a smile.
   He gave his reply to the question.

6. **hug** (verb) — to put the arms around and hold close; (noun) — a close hold with the arms
   Kath gave Alex a hug.
   Rebecca hugged her doll.

7. **sulk** (verb) — to show anger by being in a bad mood or by not speaking
   Don't sulk just because your boyfriend forgot to call.

8. **career** (noun) — a skilled, high-level job; profession
   After playing amateur sports in high school, he had a career as a baseball player for the Dodgers.

9. **dislike** (verb) — to not like; (noun) — a feeling of not liking
   She likes baseball but she dislikes football.
   Craig has a strong dislike for meat.

10. **follow** (verb)
    1) to go after
       Ruth followed her daughter up the stairs and into the house.
       A dance will follow the dinner.
    2) to go along
       Follow the yellow brick road until you come to the land of Oz.
    3) listen to, obey
       Follow these directions carefully.
    4) understand
       There were so many characters in the movie that I couldn't follow it.

11. **toward** (preposition)
    1) in the direction of
       He walked toward the door.
    2) near in time
       Toward the end of the day he began to feel sick.
    3) for
       They're saving toward a new car.

12. **brush**
    1) (noun)—an object made of stiff hair, wire, or plastic, usually with a holder, used for fixing hair, cleaning or painting; (verb)—to use a brush
       There are many kinds of brushes: hairbrushes, toothbrushes, paintbrushes, and brushes for scrubbing away dirt.
       She brushed her son's hair.
    2) (verb)—touch lightly when passing by
       His hand brushed the glass and it fell off the table.
    3) (verb)—take off
       After he fell he tried to brush the dirt from his pants.
       When she saw him coming she brushed the tears from her eyes.
    4) brush off (verb)—to not think important or not pay attention to
       I told him he was too sick to go out, but he brushed off what I said and ran outside.
       I asked my employer if I could talk to him but he brushed me off.

Idioms

Idioms are words that have special meanings in English when used together.

1. **give up**—to stop doing or stop having something
   Hoa was so sleepy that she couldn't concentrate, so she had to give up studying and go to bed.

2. **as soon as possible**—the fastest something is able to happen [see Vocabulary #1]
   Please come to my office as soon as possible.

3. **turn pale**—when a person's face becomes whiter in color, usually because of pain or surprise [see Vocabulary #2]
   He turned pale with pain when he dropped the television on his foot.

4. **times have changed**—the way people think and do things now have changed from the way they were in the past
   In 1900 most people in the United States lived on farms, but times have changed. Today most people live in cities.

5. **to make up** (past tense—*made up*)—to become friendly again after having a fight
   I hate it when we fight. Let's hug and make up.
   They made up when he said, "I'm sorry; I was selfish."

Part 2

Vocabulary

Complete each of the following sentences with one of the words on the list. Don't forget to read the words before the blank *and* the words after the blank to help you find the missing vocabulary word.

Remember that all the answers (a, b, c) under one number are different meanings of the same word. When a word has more than one meaning there is a parenthesis ( ) after the sentence. In the parenthesis put the number of the meaning from the vocabulary list in Part 1.

reply	career
hug	sulk
possible	pale
shovel	pail
brush	follow
toward	dislike

1. a) If you _____ this highway it will take you to the medical

   center. ( )

   b) The waiter said, "Please _____ me and I will take you

   to your table." ( )

   c) He talked so fast that I couldn't _____ what he was say-

   ing. ( )

   d) A soldier must _____ orders. ( )

2. He used a _____ to dig the hole.

3. a) You should _____ your teeth every morning. ( )

   b) She _____ (ed) the snow from her coat with her hand. ( )

   c) She tried to _____ him off but he kept calling her. ( )

   d) He _____ (ed) by her when he passed in the hall. ( )

4. The little girl started to _____ because her mother wouldn't let her stay up late to watch TV.

5. Esther was so happy to see her grandchildren that she gave them each a big _____.

6. President Reagan had a _____ in acting and then he had a _____ in politics.

7. I _____ winter; it's too cold.

8. a) When she saw her mother coming, she walked _____ her. ( )

   b) I am working _____ my GED. ( )

   c) It's getting _____ 11 o'clock. ( )

9. Jack and Jill went up the hill to fetch a _____ of water.

10. a) After her illness, her face was _____. ( )

    b) I want to paint the kitchen _____ yellow. ( )

11. I'm not sure, but it may be _____ for the doctor to see you if you wait.

12. I wrote Sarah a letter and now I'm waiting for her to _____.

Idioms

Complete each of the following sentences with one of the idioms on the list. Don't forget to read the words before the blank *and* the words after the blank to help you find the missing idioms.

give up   make up
times have changed   as soon as possible
turned pale

1. She gasped and _____ when she saw all the blood.

2. When I told the doctor about the piece of wood sticking into my toe, he told me to come to the hospital _____ .

3. Thirty years ago not many women in the United States worked, but _____ . Most women work now.

4. She had to _____ smoking when the doctor said it was dangerous to her health.

5. He sent her flowers because he knew she was angry and he wanted to _____ with her.

Part 3

Summary

Bradley is leaving Samantha for Gloria. Bradley gets angry at Gloria. He goes to find Samantha on the beach and sees her kissing John Paul. Gloria comes after him.

Questions to think and talk about before you read:

- Should a woman put her man before her job?
- Should a man put his job before his woman?

Episode 7. Should a Man Come First?

"Why did you follow me?" asked Bradley as he looked at Gloria standing before him on the beach.

"I'm sorry if I hurt your feelings," replied Gloria. "I didn't mean to brush you off like that."

Bradley turned his head away. "You seem to be too busy for me."

Gloria took his hand. "Bradley, I love you, but I do get busy sometimes. I have a career."

"I don't like it when a woman puts her job before me. A woman should put a man first. That's one of the things I disliked about Samantha," sulked Bradley.

Gloria smiled. "I'm not asking *you* to give up your job for *me*. Times have changed."

"But I haven't changed!" said Bradley.

"Try to understand," answered Gloria, "and I'll try to pay more attention to you." She put her arms around him and hugged him.

"Well, okay," said Bradley against her neck. "I'll try."

Gloria took his hand as they walked toward the car. "I'm glad we made up. Let's go get your things and you can move into my house today."

Bradley stopped and looked past the children with their pails and shovels toward the part of the beach where he had seen Samantha kissing John Paul. Then he turned back to Gloria.

"Fine," he answered, "I want to be out of there as soon as possible."

Samantha opened her eyes after kissing John Paul and looked across the beach. She turned pale when she saw Bradley turn around and walk away.

Part 4

Questions

1. Why did Gloria follow Bradley?
2. Why is Bradley angry?
3. What does Bradley think a woman should put first in her life?
4. What does Gloria mean, "times have changed"?
5. Does Gloria
   a) want to give up her job for Bradley?
   b) want to give up Bradley for her job?
   c) want both Bradley and her job?

6. What are Bradley and Gloria each going to do so they can go back together?
7. What is Bradley thinking about when he looks toward the part of the beach where he saw Samantha?
8. How is he feeling when he says, "I want to be out of there as soon as possible"?
9. What does Samantha see when she opens her eyes?
10. What do you think Samantha was feeling when the story says, "She turned pale when she saw Bradley turn and walk away"?

Part 5

Put the correct vocabulary word in each blank in the story. Use the words before *and* after the blank to help you find the correct vocabulary word.

possible	brush
pail	follow
pale	career
sulk	shovel
hug	toward
reply	dislike

When John refused to ＿＿＿＿＿＿ to my question, I

＿＿＿＿＿＿ (ed) him all around the house, trying to get him to talk

to me. I watched him ＿＿＿＿＿＿ his hair and put on an ugly shirt

that he knows I ＿＿＿＿＿＿. When he picked up his snow ＿＿＿＿＿

and walked ＿＿＿＿＿＿ the door to go out I started to ＿＿＿＿＿＿

and I went to my room and wouldn't come out. When he saw me go

into my room he went into the kitchen and filled up a ＿＿＿＿＿＿ of

water and started washing the floor. When I heard him singing, "It's

not a job, it's a ＿＿＿＿＿＿ in the army," I knew it would probably

not be ＿＿＿＿＿＿ to stop him from joining the army, and that was the answer to my question. When I heard him at my door saying, "You really should come out," I opened the door. As I looked at his handsome _____ face, I knew he would go. I put my arms around him and gave him a _____ .

Part 6

There are eight vocabulary words spelled incorrectly in this copy of the story. Find the mistakes and correct them. The first one has been done for you.

follow
"Why did you ~~folow~~ me?" asked Bradley as he looked at Gloria standing before him on the beach.

"I'm sorry if I hurt your feelings," replied Gloria. "I didn't mean to brush you off like that."

Bradley turned his head away. "You seem to be too busy for me."

Gloria took his hand. "Bradley, I love you, but I do get busy sometimes. I have a carreer."

"I don't like it when a woman puts her job before me. A woman should put a man first. That's one of the things I desliked about Samantha," solked Bradley.

Gloria smiled. "I'm not asking *you* to give up your job for *me*. Times have changed."

"But I haven't changed!" said Bradley.

"Try to understand," answered Gloria, "and I'll try to pay more attention to you." She put her arms around him and hugged him.

"Well, okay," said Bradley against her neck. "I'll try."

Gloria took his hand as they walked toard the car. "I'm glad we made up. Let's go get your things and you can move into my house today."

Bradley stopped and looked past the children with their pales and shovels toward the part of the beach where he had seen Samantha kissing John Paul. Then he turned back to Gloria.

"Fine," he answered, "I want to be out of there as soon as posible."

Samantha opened her eyes after kissing John Paul and looked across the beach. She turned pail when she saw Bradley turn around and walk away.

Chapter 8

Should She or Shouldn't She?

Should She or Shouldn't She?

Part 1

Vocabulary

These are the vocabulary words you will learn in this chapter. Each word has a definition and a sentence. Notice that many words have more than one meaning.

1. **voice** (noun)—sound made in speaking or singing
   He knew from the sound of her voice that she was furious with him.

2. **offend** (verb)—to make someone sad or angry, insult
   Using bad language and speaking rudely may offend people.

3. **indecisive** (adjective)—not sure, not able to make a decision;
   indecisively (adverb)
   She was indecisive over whether to buy this perfume or that one.
   "I don't know what to do," he said indecisively.

4. **exclaim** (verb)—to speak with excitement or surprise
   *"How could you withdraw all of the money from our joint account
       without telling me!" exclaimed Peter.*
   The women started to exclaim over the new baby.

5. **quick** (adjective); **quickly** (adverb)
   1) fast
      Let's have a quick sandwich before we go to school.
      He gets mad easily. He has a quick temper.
      Polish the car quickly because we have to leave soon.
   2) fast in being able to understand
      He's intelligent and quick in his studies.

6. **urgent** (adjective)—something of great importance that needs to be done quickly

    I have an urgent letter for Ms. Jefferson.

7. **puzzle**
    1) (noun)—something difficult to understand; (verb)—to make difficult to understand; **puzzled** (adjective)—not able to understand

        It's a puzzle to me how we can waste so much money.

        Your sad sighs puzzle me.

        He knew she didn't understand because she gave him a puzzled look.

    2) (noun)—a game that is hard to do

        A jigsaw puzzle is a picture that is cut into pieces and you must put the pieces back together.

8. **hardly** (adverb)—almost not at all

    After paying the rent I had hardly any money left.

9. **grab** (verb)
    1) to take quickly

        I have to grab my books and leave or I'll be late for school.

        When they asked George if he wanted the free tickets, he grabbed at the chance.

    2) to take quickly, by force

        The little girl tried to grab the toy away from her brother.

10. **abrupt** (adjective); **abruptly** (adverb)
    1) sudden

        Her singing career came to an abrupt end when she had an operation on her throat.

        I'm sorry to stop your meeting so abruptly, but one of your employees has had a bad accident.

    2) not polite

        He offended me when he gave me such an abrupt answer to my question.

        He ended our appointment so abruptly that I knew he would never give me the job.

11. **cry**
    1) (verb) — to have tears come out of the eyes; (noun) — a period of crying
       He felt so bad when he got dismissed from his job that he cried.
       When I'm depressed I feel better after a good cry.
    2) (verb) — to call out loudly; (noun) — a loud call, yell
       "Veronica is in first place!" cried Elvira as she watched the race.
       When we heard his cry for help we knew he was in trouble.

12. **desperate** (adjective) — causing great need or worry; being willing to do anything to get what one wants; **desperately** (adverb)
    Because he hadn't eaten for three days, he felt a desperate need for food.
    She is in desperate trouble.
    When she saw that the whole room was on fire, she ran desperately toward the door.

Idioms

Idioms are words that have special meanings in English when used together.

1. **stop by** — go, usually for a short time
   I need to stop by the gym and get my sneakers.
   Will you be home after work? I thought I'd stop by.

2. **his lips met hers** — his lips touched her lips; they kissed
   When her lips met his, she knew it was love.

3. **so what?** — showing that you don't care about something or that it is not important
   More people came to the party than we expected, but so what? We have plenty of food.

4. **get to know** — begin to know
   Traveling to different parts of the United States is a good way to get to know this country.

5. **hold back** (past tense — *held back*) — stay or keep back, showing you don't want to do something
   Because she dislikes being first, she always holds back when the others jump in the water.
   She held back her answer to give the others a chance to reply.

6. **little while** — short time
   I've only known him for a little while.

Part 2

Vocabulary

Complete each of the following sentences with one of the vocabulary words on the list. Don't forget to read the words before the blank *and* the words after the blank to help you find the missing vocabulary word.

   Remember that all of the answers (a, b, c) under one number are different meanings of the same word. When a word has more than one meaning, there is a parenthesis ( ) after the sentence. In the parenthesis put the number of the meaning from the vocabulary list in Part 1.

urgent	abrupt
quick	exclaim
cry	offend
hardly	desperate
voice	puzzle
indecisive	grab

1. Because she had a sore throat her ＿＿＿＿＿＿ sounded funny on the phone.

2. a) When babies are hungry, they ＿＿＿＿＿＿. ( )

   b) He gave a loud ＿＿＿＿＿＿ when he saw the police taking away his car. ( )

3. Tell George to call his wife right away. It's ＿＿＿＿＿＿.

4. a) I don't like that bank; the service there is too _____. ( )

   b) My vacation came to an _____ stop when someone stole all my money. ( )

5. a) I have a 300-piece _____ to put together. ( )

   b) I don't understand the way she's acting. It _____ (s) me. ( )

6. a) He was in a hurry so he walked _____ (ly). ( )

   b) She has a _____ mind. ( )

7. a) When the glass fell off the table, she _____ (bed) it before it hit the floor. ( )

   b) As she was walking through the park recently, a man _____ (bed) her bag and ran away with it. ( )

8. You will _____ your sister if you wear a t-shirt and jeans to her wedding.

9. Because she was so _____ it took her a long time to decide what to wear.

10. When she found out her child was missing, she felt _____.

11. With the lights out, I can _____ see.

12. "Our team beat the other team by 20 points!" _____ (ed) Laura.

Idioms

Complete each of the following sentences with one of the idioms on the list. Don't forget to read the words before the blank *and* the words after the blank to help you find the missing idioms.

so what?	his lips met hers
get to know	stop by
holds back	little while

1. I know Lisa is mad at me, but _____ I never liked her anyway!

2. He put his arms around her waist, _____, and they kissed.

3. A shy person _____ his feelings.

4. Now that I am in the same class as Martha, I hope to _____ _____ her better.

5. Can you _____ the store and buy a shovel for the garden?

6. I can only stop by your house for a _____ and then I have to go to work.

Part 3

Summary

Bradley is leaving Samantha for Gloria. Bradley and Gloria fight and make up. Samantha meets John Paul on the beach and knows that Bradley has seen her kissing John Paul.

Questions to think and talk about before you read:

- How do you think Samantha will feel now that she knows Bradley has seen her with John Paul?
- Do you think it's okay for Samantha to kiss John Paul?

Episode 8. Should She or Shouldn't She?

"I have to leave now," said Samantha abruptly to John Paul as they stood on the beach together. She knew Bradley had seen them kissing.

"Why?" asked John Paul, putting his arms around her. "We're

having such a nice time." As he bent down to kiss her again, she pushed him away and said, "I want to go, now!"

"What's so urgent?" asked John Paul in a puzzled voice. "You were fine just a minute ago."

"I'll see you sometime at the hospital," she said. She started to walk quickly away but he grabbed her hand.

"What happened?" he asked. "Did I do something to offend you?"

"No," she replied, turning away from him. "I just shouldn't be here."

"Then let's go," he said, walking with her. "Come home with me."

"Come home with you!" exclaimed Samantha, staring at him. "I hardly know you!"

"You could get to know me better," he said, bringing her closer.

"I shouldn't," said Samantha, as he put his arms around her. "I couldn't," she said as his lips met hers. "I'm a married woman!" cried Samantha desperately, pulling away.

"So what?" answered John Paul. "Your husband is doing the same thing. Come to my house with me. Anyway, we won't do anything; we'll just talk."

"Well . . ." said Samantha indecisively. "I could stop by for just a minute . . ."

"Okay," said John Paul, pulling her along. "Let's go."

But Samantha held back. "I do have a lot of things to do at home. Maybe another time."

"Come on," said John Paul softly as he looked into her eyes. "Just for a little while."

"Well . . ." said Samantha.

Part 4

Questions

1. Why does Samantha want to leave? How do you think she's feeling?
2. Why is John Paul puzzled? How is Samantha acting toward him?
3. Where does John Paul want Samantha to go?
4. Give one reason Samantha has for not going with John Paul.
5. What does John Paul mean when he says, "We won't do anything; we'll just talk"?

6. Did you believe John Paul when he says that he and Samantha will just talk at his house? Why or why not?

7. In your opinion, is it okay for Samantha to go with John Paul or is it wrong?

8. In your opinion, does Samantha go with John Paul or not?

Part 5

Fill in the blanks next to each definition with your vocabulary words. Then put the words together in the blanks that follow and see what the sentence says!

1. not able to understand   _____ (ed)

2. very important, needing attention quickly   _____

3. sound of speaking   _____

4. willing to do anything because of great need   _____

5. sudden   _____

6. when tears come out of the eyes   _____

7. in a fast way   _____ (ly)

8. spoke with excitement   _____ (ed)

9. to take quickly   _____

10. almost not at all   _____

11. not sure   _____

12. make angry, insult   _____

I was 1) _____ by an 2) _____ 3) _____ ,

4) _____ and 5) _____ , that gave a 6) _____ and

7) _____ 8) _____ , "If you 9) _____ you're

10) _____ 11) _____ , but you may 12) _____ !"

Part 6

There are eight vocabulary words spelled incorrectly in this copy of the story. Find the mistakes and correct them. The first one has been done for you.

                         abruptly
    "I have to leave now," said Samantha ~~abruply~~ to John Paul as they stood on the beach together. She knew Bradley had seen them kissing.

    "Why?" asked John Paul, putting his arms around her. "We're having such a nice time." As he bent down to kiss her again, she pushed him away and said, "I want to go, now!"

    "What's so urgant?" asked John Paul in a puzled voice. "You were fine just a minute ago."

    "I'll see you sometime at the hospital," she said. She started to walk quikly away but he grabbed her hand.

    "What happened?" he asked. "Did I do something to ofend you?"

    "No," she replied, turning away from him. "I just shouldn't be here."

    "Then let's go," he said, walking with her. "Come home with me."

    "Come home with you!" exclaimed Samantha, staring at him. "I hardly know you!"

    "You could get to know me better," he said, bringing her closer.

    "I shouldn't," said Samantha, as he put his arms around her. "I couldn't," she said as his lips met hers. "I'm a married woman!" cried Samantha desperetely, pulling away.

    "So what?" answered John Paul. "Your husband is doing the same thing. Come to my house with me. Anyway, we won't do anything; we'll just talk."

"Well . . ." said Samantha indesisively. "I could stop by for just a minute . . ."

"Okay," said John Paul, pulling her along. "Let's go."

But Samantha held back. "I do have a lot of things to do at home. Maybe another time."

"Come on," said John Paul softly as he looked into her eyes. "Just for a little while."

"Well . . ." said Samantha.

Chapter 9

Life Is So Complicated

Chapter 9

Life Is So Complicated

Part 1

Vocabulary

These are the vocabulary words you will learn in this chapter. Each word has a definition and a sentence. Notice that many words have more than one meaning.

1. **ought** (verb, used with "to")—should, to be responsible for
   You ought to get your mother a present for Mother's Day.

2. **frown** (verb)—to look sad or angry by bringing the eyebrows together in a look of sadness or anger
   Peter frowned when he heard the bad news.
   "Please don't bother me now!" Sheila said with a frown.

3. **blush**
   1) (verb)—to turn red in the face because a person feels nervous or silly; (noun)—a redness out of nervousness
      When he grabbed her hand and told her he loved her, she blushed.
      When she asked Al his name, a blush came over his face.
   2) (noun)—a red or pink color; makeup of a red or pink color
      There was a blush in the sky as the sun began to rise.
      Iris wanted her cheeks to look pink, so she used blush.

4. **react** (verb)—to do, say, or behave in answer to something that has happened
   When her mother yelled at her, the girl reacted by running out of the house.

5. **personal** (adjective)
   1) private, belonging to that person
      The things in my desk are my personal property; please don't touch them.
      His personal questions offended me.
   2) in person, not done by anyone else but that person
      The famous baseball player made a personal visit to the children in the hospital.

6. **calm** (adjective)—quiet, peaceful; (noun)—quietness, peacefulness; (verb)—to make quiet and peaceful
   The sea is calm tonight.
   The water and the wind are quiet now, but it's the calm before the storm.
   Children, you're too wild. Please calm down.

7. **forward**
   1) (adjective)—near or at the front; (adverb)—toward the front
      Please leave the plane by the forward door.
      When they called Jali's name, she came forward.
   2) (adjective)—bold, pushing ahead, advanced
      The boss liked his new, forward ideas.
      He was forward with the girls.
   3) (verb)—to send ahead
      If the letter comes to my work address, please forward it to me at home.

8. **concern**
   1) (noun)—troubled interest, worry; **concerned** (adjective)—worried; (verb)—to trouble or worry
      The boy's bad grades were of enormous concern to his parents.
      She was concerned that her new outfit would get ruined in the rain.
      It concerns me when you come home so late.
   2) (verb)—to be about, to have importance to; (noun)—something of importance or interest
      This story concerns two old men.
      Anything my daughter does is of concern to me.

9. **conscious** (adjective)
   1) aware, knowing about
      She was conscious that her son was sulking after she told him he couldn't go out.
   2) definite, planned
      Because he didn't want Janel to know he was watching her, he made a conscious effort to look surprised when she waved to him.
   3) awake
      When she became conscious after the accident she saw that she was lying in the middle of the street.

10. **complicated**
    1) (adjective)—not simple, hard to understand, having many parts
       Learning a new language is complicated.
    2) (verb, past tense of *to complicate*)—worsened one medical problem with another
       The difficulty of the operation was complicated by the patient's breathing problems.

11. **except** (preposition)—all but some, other than
    We have everything we brought to the beach except the pail and shovel. They must be lost.
    I don't take orders from anyone except the boss.
    I would go, except it's too far.

12. **accept** (verb)
    1) to take something that is given to you
       Because I wasn't home, my neighbor accepted the package for me.
    2) to agree to, believe in
       The teacher accepted the doctor's note as an excuse for her absence.
       Will you accept the charges for a long distance call?
       I can't accept your ideas.

Idioms

Idioms are words that have special meanings in English when used together.

1. **run into**—meet without planning to
   Rosa ran into Linda at the copy machine.

2. **what is it?**—what's the problem?
   I heard that Laura was desperate to speak to me. What is it?

3. **head in his hands**—when a person leans his head on his hands because he is upset or worried
   "What will I do now? Where will I go?" she sighed indecisively with her head in her hands.

Part 2

Vocabulary

Complete each of the following sentences with one of the vocabulary words on the list. Don't forget to read the words before the blank *and* the words after the blank to help you find the missing vocabulary word.

Remember that all of the answers (a, b, c) under one number are different meanings of the same word. When a word has more than one meaning, there is a parenthesis ( ) after the sentence. In the parenthesis put the number of the meaning from the vocabulary list in Part 1.

concern	complicated
personal	calm
blush	forward
conscious	react
accept	ought
except	frown

1. a) This has nothing to do with you. It does not _____

   you. ( )

b) When Mary found out that George was in the hospital she

showed her ＿＿＿＿＿＿ by going to visit him. ( )

2. a) He was ＿＿＿＿＿＿ of a strange smell in the room. ( )

b) After the operation we waited until she became ＿＿＿＿＿＿

so that we could visit her. ( )

c) He made a ＿＿＿＿＿＿ decision to be nice to his sister. ( )

3. a) The directions are so ＿＿＿＿＿＿ I can't understand them. ( )

b) Her heart disease was ＿＿＿＿＿＿ by other medical

problems. ( )

4. Everyone is going to the party ＿＿＿＿＿＿ Maria; she has to

work.

5. a) Please ＿＿＿＿＿＿ this money to help pay your expenses. ( )

b) I can't ＿＿＿＿＿＿ what you're saying to me; it's something I

can't believe. ( )

6. People smile when they're happy and ＿＿＿＿＿＿ when they're

sad.

7. I know I ＿＿＿＿＿＿ to clean the house, but I feel like sleeping

instead.

8. The soft music made him feel very ＿＿＿＿＿＿.

9. a) When she saw that everyone was looking at her, she

＿＿＿＿＿＿ (ed). ( )

b) Some women use ＿＿＿＿＿＿, makeup that makes their

cheeks pink. ( )

10. a) The conversation between my husband and me is private and

＿＿＿＿＿＿. ( )

b) The governor made a ＿＿＿＿＿＿ visit to our school. ( )

11. When you touch something hot, you _____ by pulling your hand away.

12. a) When she moved, she asked the post office to _____ the mail to her new address. ( )

    b) The people in line behind Eric followed him when he moved _____ . ( )

    c) Although I didn't know him well, I was so troubled that I was very _____ in telling him my problem. ( )

Idioms

Complete each of the following sentences with one of the idioms on the list. Don't forget to read the words before the blank *and* the words after the blank to find the missing idiom.

    ran into
    what is it
    head in his hands

1. I was surprised when I _____ Barbara at the supermarket this morning.

2. When the doctor told him his son was dying, he turned pale, put his _____ , and started to cry.

3. I got an urgent message from you. _____ ?

Part 3

Summary

Bradley has left Samantha for Gloria. Samantha meets John Paul on the beach.

Questions to think and talk about before you read:

- What kind of person do you think John Paul is?
- Do you think Samantha will be happier with him than with Bradley?

Episode 9. Life Is So Complicated

It was Monday. Samantha was surprised to find that she was glad to get to work. She was conscious of wanting to be busy so she could forget about her personal life for a while. The beginning of the day was really busy and she forgot about everything except work until lunchtime.

In the hospital lunch room she looked around for Jasmine and David. David, Samantha, and Jasmine had been friends since they all began working in the hospital two years before. She saw them at a table against the wall.

As they all started eating, David asked, "What happened with you and Bradley? Does he still have that girlfriend?"

"Yes," said Samantha with a frown. "He moved all of his things out of the house yesterday and moved in with Gloria."

"You must be upset," said David with concern.

"Well, yes and no," answered Samantha.

"He was never that good to you anyway," said Jasmine. "You ought to find yourself someone else."

"Maybe I already have."

"Really? Who?" exclaimed David. They both leaned forward.

"Yesterday on the beach I ran into John Paul French, the new doctor. We had quite a nice time together." Samantha blushed.

"John Paul! Oh no!" exclaimed Jasmine.

"What is it?" asked Samantha.

"He's a friend of my husband's," answered Jasmine in a calmer voice. "He often comes to our house for dinner. The kids really like him."

"Then why did you react like that?" asked Samantha, worried.

"It's nothing, really," answered Jasmine. She looked at David.

"I can't accept that," continued Samantha. "Tell me. After all, you are my friends."

"Well," said Jasmine, "you know that blond nurse in the X-ray department? Well, I heard that she and John Paul . . . I mean, I'm not sure, but . . ." She looked at David again.

"I did see them leaving the hospital together once, but that doesn't mean anything, really," said David. No one spoke for a minute as Jasmine, David, and Samantha looked at each other.

"Oh," sighed Samantha with her head in her hands, "life is so complicated."

Part 4

Questions

1. Why was Samantha glad to get to work?
2. Where does she work?
3. Who are Jasmine and David?
4. Where did Bradley go?
5. Is Samantha upset?
6. What does Jasmine say when Samantha tells her and David about John Paul?
7. What did Jasmine hear about John Paul?
8. What did David see?
9. How is Samantha feeling when she says, "Life is so complicated?"

Part 5

Look back at the word list to help you find and circle the twelve vocabulary words in the puzzle. There are two extra words, *surprise* and *beginning*. See if you can find all fourteen words. One word has been done for you.

```
P M L D K P V T P N S N R P C
F O R W A R D R S R F R P M O
O Y W B G D F E K E D C U P M
N X H M V J U L T C S B P T P
R Q I P P O S R N N T U S O L
T P E C C A B G H O J K E L I
I M I G O C F E X C E P T M C
R K L H N D E B G A J H F C A
P L J A S U R P R I S E D R T
B P O N C P E R S O N A L C E
C Y T S I O U G H T F N A N D
A Z W U O V P L M B T E I R S
R E H S U L B A B F R O W N P
P F D C S N O M S R P T S B G
```

Part 6

There are nine vocabulary words spelled incorrectly in this copy of the story. Find the mistakes and correct them. The first one has been done for you.

It was Monday. Samantha was surprised to find that she was glad to get to work. She was ~~concious~~ conscious of wanting to be busy so she could forget about her personel life for a while. The beginning of the day was really busy and she forgot about everything exsept work until lunchtime.

In the hospital lunch room she looked around for Jasmine and David. David, Samantha, and Jasmine had been friends since they all began working in the hospital two years before. She saw them at a table against the wall.

As they all started eating, David asked, "What happened with you and Bradley? Does he still have that girlfriend?"

"Yes," said Samantha with a froun. "He moved all of his things out of the house yesterday and moved in with Gloria."

"You must be upset," said David with consern.

"Well, yes and no," answered Samantha.

"He was never that good to you anyway," said Jasmine. "You oght to find yourself someone else."

"Maybe I already have."

"Really? Who?" exclaimed David. They both leaned forward.

"Yesterday on the beach I ran into John Paul French, the new doctor. We had quite a nice time together." Samantha blushed.

"John Paul! Oh no!" exclaimed Jasmine.

"What is it?" asked Samantha.

"He's a friend of my husband's," answered Jasmine in a camer voice. "IIe often comes to our house for dinner. The kids really like him."

"Then why did you reac like that?" asked Samantha, worried.

"It's nothing, really," answered Jasmine. She looked at David.

"I can't acept that," continued Samantha. "Tell me. After all, you are my friends."

"Well," said Jasmine, "you know that blond nurse in the X-ray department? Well, I heard that she and John Paul . . . I mean, I'm not sure, but . . ." She looked at David again.

"I did see them leaving the hospital together once, but that doesn't mean anything, really," said David. No one spoke for a minute as Jasmine, David, and Samantha looked at each other.

"Oh," sighed Samantha with her head in her hands, "life is so complicated."

Chapter 10

Another Woman

Chapter *10*

Another Woman

Part 1

Vocabulary

These are the vocabulary words you will learn in this chapter. Each word has a definition and a sentence. Notice that many words have more than one meaning.

1. **embarrass** (verb)—to feel nervous or silly in front of other people
    Because she was so shy, it embarrassed her to speak in front of the class.

2. **lovely** (adjective)—beautiful, nice
    We ought to ask her to sing at the party because she has a lovely voice.
    Bringing Maria flowers was a lovely idea.

3. **rumor** (noun)—information that people tell each other that may or may not be true, gossip; (verb)—to tell a rumor
    Donna heard a rumor that school may be closed tomorrow. Sherrie told it to me and I told it to Chris, but we're waiting to find out if it's true.
    It's rumored that she brushed him off when he asked her to the dance.

4. **finally** (adverb)—at the end, at last
    The baby finally stopped crying when I gave him a bottle.

5. **date**
1) (noun)—the day, month and year; (verb)—to put on a day, month or year
What is today's date?
Don't forget to date your application.
2) (noun)—a sweet, brown fruit that grows on a palm tree
I'm going to put dates in the coffee cake.
3) (noun)—appointment to meet, especially between a man and a woman, a person of the opposite sex a man or woman meets; (verb)—to see a person of the opposite sex in a regular way, to go out with [see Idioms, #1]
Everyone has a date for Saturday night except George.
Her date's name is Jack.
Nancy hadn't been dating Rick long when they decided to get married.

6. **squeeze**
1) (verb)—to press or push hard on both sides; (noun)—a press or push on both sides
Kayla squeezed the lemon, mixed it with water and sugar, and made lemonade.
When the little boy hugged his sister, he squeezed her too hard and she began to cry.
Adrian gave his mother's hand a squeeze to show her that he understood.
2) (verb)—to push between, or into a small space; (noun)—a push between, or into a small space
The little girl squeezed between her parents on the bench.
Getting into these shoes will be a tight squeeze.

7. **else**
1) (adjective)—other, different; (adverb)—in a different way
I'm afraid my boyfriend loves somebody else.
If you don't like milk, I can get you something else.
If we don't go by bus, how else can we get there?
2) (adjective)—more; (adverb)—in addition
If you need anything else, just call me.
I've told you everything I know about it; what else do you want?
After we see the park, where else do you want to go?

8. **confuse** (verb)—to mix up in your mind, to mistake one thing for another; **confused** (adjective)—mixed up in your mind
   They always confuse me with my sister because we look so much alike.
   Samuel looked confused as he tried to put the complicated puzzle together.

9. **serious** (adjective)
   1) meaning what you say, not fooling
      To show he was serious about his concern for her, he sent a dozen roses to the hospital.
   2) having importance, not taking casually or lightly
      He's serious about his girlfriend. He wants to marry her.
   3) bad or dangerous
      The problems of the homeless are serious.
   4) causing deep thought or feeling; thoughtful
      Ulysses looked serious as he watched the movie about World War II.

10. **relax** (verb)
    1) to make loose or less tight
       I had hardly started to rub his back, when I began to feel his muscles relax.
    2) to make less strict
       When I relaxed my diet over Christmas, I gained five pounds.
    3) to rest, to become less nervous
       Calm music helps me relax.

11. **possessive** (adjective)—wanting to own or have power over someone or something
    Her possessive boyfriend wouldn't let her go anywhere without him.

12. **care**
    1) (verb)—to be interested in, concerned about; (noun)—interest, attention
       I care about how my house looks.
       "I don't care what you do," he said with a frown.
       Please handle with care.

2) (verb)—to like or love

She blushed when her boyfriend said, "You know how much I care for you."

3) (verb)—to watch over, protect; (noun)—protection

If I leave, who will care for the children?

Take care of your sister.

Idioms

1. **go out with**—to go somewhere with another person for fun, especially a person of the opposite sex; to date [see Vocabulary #5]

Lisa would like to go out with Michael.

2. **seeing each other**—can be used to mean a man and a woman who see each other in a regular way, who are going out with each other, dating [see Idioms #1 and Vocabulary #5]

Paul and Denise have been seeing each other for several months.

3. **throw back his head and laugh**—give such a big laugh that a person's whole body and head goes back and then comes forward as he laughs

When she heard the joke she threw back her head and laughed.

4. **to say so**—to say that

She knows what she wants, and she says so.

I believe it's possible for there to be people on other planets, and I said so in front of everyone.

Part 2

Vocabulary

Complete each of the following sentences with one of the vocabulary words on the list. Don't forget to read the words before the blank *and* the words after the blank to help you find the missing vocabulary word.

Remember that all of the answers (a, b, c) under one number are different meanings of the same word. When a word has more than one meaning, there is a parenthesis ( ) after the sentence. In the parenthesis put the number of the meaning from the vocabulary list in Part 1.

date	else
embarrass	finally
possessive	serious
relax	confuse
squeeze	lovely
rumor	care

1. a) After a hard day at work, I like to _____ in front of the TV. ( )

b) The boy was so scared that he wouldn't _____ his hold on his mother. ( )

c) When the children began to behave better, their mother decided to _____ some of the rules. ( )

2. a) He took _____ of his sick mother. ( )

b) She does a good job because she _____ (s) about her work. ( )

c) I gave you this valentine to show how much I _____ for you. ( )

3. a) To make orange juice, you have to _____ the oranges. ( )

b) Because it was the only car we had, we had to _____ eight people into it. ( )

4. The girl felt _____ (ed) when she fell down and everybody laughed.

5. I heard a _____ that Mary is getting married, but I don't know if it's true.

6. Let's go outside. It's a _____ day for a walk.

7. It took me an hour to find the answer to the teacher's complicated question, but I _____ got it.

8. The streets and buildings of the big city _____ (d) him and

he got lost.

9. a) He isn't joking; he's very _____. ( )

b) She had to go to the hospital because she had a _____

illness. ( )

c) Graduation from high school is a _____ time in a per-

son's life. ( )

d) Smile, it's a party. Don't be so _____. ( )

10. He's _____ about his car. He won't let anyone else drive it.

11. a) Linda and Francisco have a _____ to go to the movies

together. ( )

b) Israel ate three of the sweet _____ (s). ( )

c) July 12 is the _____ of their anniversary. ( )

12. a) Have you had enough to eat, or do you want something

_____ ? ( )

b) I'm too tired to go to the store. Can you ask somebody

_____ ? ( )

Idioms

Complete each of the following sentences with one of the idioms on the
list. Don't forget to read the words before the blank *and* the words after the blank to help you find the missing idioms.

say so
go out with
threw back his head and laughed
see her

1. If I ask Elena to _____ me, do you think she'll

accept?

2. After Jorge had a fight with his girlfriend, he told her he didn't

   want to _____ anymore.

3. I know Mary doesn't like Timothy, but it wasn't nice of her to

   _____ in front of him.

4. I guess he thought my question was funny, because he

   _____ .

Part 3

Summary

Bradley has left Samantha for Gloria. Samantha goes out with John Paul and then finds out from her friends David and Jasmine that he may be seeing another woman.

Questions to think and talk about before you read:

- If Samantha thinks John Paul is seeing someone else, what should she do about it?
- If she wants to talk to John Paul about it, is it okay for her to call him?

Episode 10. Another Woman

Samantha couldn't relax. She turned the TV on and turned it off. She sat in the living room and then in the kitchen. All she could think about was what Jasmine and David had told her about John Paul. Was he really going out with someone else? Did he really care about her? Finally she went to the phone.

"John Paul?" she said into the phone. "This is Samantha. Would you like to go out for a drink? I'd like to talk to you."

Later that evening Samantha and John Paul sat in the Beacon Bar. "You look lovely tonight," said John Paul, taking her hand. "I was so glad you called."

"How nice of you to say so," said Samantha, squeezing his hand. "Knowing that makes it easier for me to talk to you."

"What do you want to talk to me about?" asked John Paul.

"Well," said Samantha, looking down at the table, a little embarrassed, "I heard a rumor about you at the hospital."

"A rumor? About me?" asked John Paul, surprised. "What did it say?"

"That you're dating the blond nurse in the X-ray department," said Samantha nervously.

John Paul threw back his head and started to laugh. "Is that all! I thought it was something really terrible."

Samantha looked confused. "But is it true?"

"Well, yes," answered John Paul, "I go out with her sometimes, so what?"

"But you're going out with me!" cried Samantha.

John Paul looked surprised. "I see her, and I see you. What's wrong with that?"

"But you never told me that!" said Samantha. "The way you look at me and talk to me, I thought . . ."

John Paul laughed again. "Don't you think it's too soon to be getting so possessive? I never gave you the idea that we were serious."

"But . . ." said Samantha.

"Oh come on," said John Paul, pulling her close to him. "Don't be so serious. Let's just have a good time."

Samantha felt sick to her stomach. She stood up and ran out of the bar.

Part 4

Questions

1. Why does Samantha turn the TV on and off? Why can't she relax?
2. What does she finally do?
3. At the bar, what is the rumor Samantha tells John Paul about?
4. How does John Paul react when she tells him about the rumor?
5. Does John Paul think what he's doing is wrong?
6. What does John Paul think Samantha is doing too soon?
7. How does Samantha feel at the end?
8. Who do you think is right, John Paul or Samantha? Why?

9. In your country is it okay for a man or woman to date more than one person? Is it okay in the U.S.?

Part 5

Use your vocabulary words to complete this crossword puzzle.

Across

1. What you do when you put your feet up and close your eyes
2. How you feel when you drop your books in the classroom and everyone is looking at you (+ ed)
3. All mixed up in your mind
4. A time to meet your girlfriend
5. At last
6. What you do to an orange to make juice
7. The opposite of joking

Down

1. When someone tells you something she heard from someone else who heard it from someone else who heard it from . . .
3. To like someone very much
8. When you want something all for yourself
9. Beautiful
10. Something more is something _____

Part 6

There are eight vocabulary words spelled incorrectly in this copy of the story. Find the mistakes and correct them. The first one has been done for you.

Samantha couldn't relax. She turned the TV on and turned it off. She sat in the living room and then in the kitchen. All she could think about was what Jasmine and David had told her about John Paul. Was he really going out with someone else? Did he really care about her? Finally
~~Finaly~~ she went to the phone.

"John Paul?" she said into the phone. "This is Samantha. Would you like to go out for a drink? I'd like to talk to you."

Later that evening Samantha and John Paul sat in the Beacon Bar. "You look lovly tonight," said John Paul, taking her hand. "I was so glad you called."

"How nice of you to say so," said Samantha, sqeezing his hand. "Knowing that makes it easier for me to talk to you."

"What do you want to talk to me about?" asked John Paul.

"Well," said Samantha, looking down at the table, a little embarased, "I heard a roomor about you at the hospital."

"A rumor? About me?" asked John Paul, surprised. "What did it say?"

"That you're dating the blond nurse in the X-ray department," said Samantha nervously.

John Paul threw back his head and started to laugh. "Is that all! I thought it was something really terrible."

Samantha looked confuced. "But is it true?"

"Well, yes," answered John Paul, "I go out with her sometimes, so what?"

"But you're going out with me!" cried Samantha.

John Paul looked surprised. "I see her, and I see you. What's wrong with that?"

"But you never told me that!" said Samantha. "The way you look at me and talk to me, I thought . . ."

John Paul laughed again. "Don't you think it's too soon to be getting so posesive? I never gave you the idea that we were serios."

"But . . ." said Samantha.

"Oh come on," said John Paul, pulling her close to him. "Don't be so serious. Let's just have a good time."

Samantha felt sick to her stomach. She stood up and ran out of the bar.

Dating in the United States

Part 1

Questions to think and talk about before you read:

- What is dating like in your country?

In different countries men and women meet and get to know each other in different ways. In some countries men and women who are not married can see each other only if other family members are also there. In some countries the parents of young men and women *arrange*, or plan, their children's marriages and the young people may meet only once, or not at all, before their wedding. In some countries people accept a man going out with more than one woman, but not a woman going out with more than one man. It may be difficult for people from other countries to get used to the dating *customs*, or regular way of doing things, in the United States.

In the United States men and women choose who they want to go out with. They may meet each other through family or friends, at school, their place of work, at a party, or even at a bar. The regular way of doing things that is *common* or usual in recent years is for some people to meet at singles bars or singles dances. These are places where single, unmarried people go to meet people of the opposite sex. Some singles parties are given by churches, synagogues, or schools and almost everyone believes that these are good places to meet other people. Many people do not agree that singles bars are safe places to meet new people.

Sometimes a person will *arrange* or plan a date between two people she knows who have never met but who she thinks might like each other. For example, Larry has two friends, Joel and Nora, who do not know each other. He asks each of them if they would like to go on a date together to see if they like each other. Since they are going out without ever seeing each other before, this is called a *blind date*. To make it easier for them Larry might arrange for Joel and Nora to go somewhere with Larry and his girlfriend. Because there are then two men and two women on the date, this is called a *double date*.

A man and a woman may go out by themselves, on a double date, or in a group. A lot of the time it is *common* for people on a date to go to the movies, a restaurant, or a party, but a date can also be to a beach, for a bicycle ride, or anywhere that one person invites another to go.

Usually it is the man who asks the woman out, and the man pays for the movie or the food or whatever is done on the date. Among some people this is changing, and the woman will sometimes pay half of the cost, especially when the two people have been dating for a while.

In the United States it is quite *common* for a man or woman to date more than one person at the same time. For example, a woman may go to a party with one man on Friday, to the movies with a different man on Saturday, and out to dinner with a third man a week later. This is looked at as normal and not bad at all as long as she makes it clear to all three men that she is dating more than one person. This changes once the two people become more serious about each other and agree not to date other people. The man would then expect his girlfriend to see only him and his girlfriend would expect the same. Problems come up between two people who are dating, as with John Paul and Samantha, when one person is less serious and wants to date other people, and the other person wants him to be her boyfriend and see only her.

When two people are serious about each other they may decide to get married, and this is called *getting engaged.* It is the custom for the man to give the woman an engagement ring at this time to show that they are *engaged* and plan to be married. When two people are serious about each other for a while but then decide not to stay together, that is called *breaking up.*

We will see what happens with the dating between John Paul and Samantha. Will they become more serious or will they *break up?*

Part 2

Questions

1. Name two places where men and women in the United States meet each other.
2. Who usually gives singles parties?
3. Name two places that a man and a woman usually go on a date.
4. Who usually asks for a date, and who pays?
5. In the United States, is it wrong for a man to date more than one woman or a woman to date more than one man?
6. When does this change?
7. When is this a problem?

Part 3

Vocabulary and Idioms

There are a few new words and idioms in what you have just read. You should be able to understand the meanings of these words by reading the words *before* and *after* them. Usually the definition of the word or idiom is in the same sentence as the word or idiom.

Fill in the blanks with the words that go with the definition. If there are two blanks next to a definition, it is because there are two words with the same definition. If you're not sure of the meaning of the words, look back at the story.

common	blind date
arrange	double date
custom	get engaged
break up	

1. plan   _____

2. regular way of doing things   _____

                                                 _____

3. a date with someone you've never seen before _____

4. a date for two men and two women   _____

5. to decide to get married   _____

6. to decide not to see each other any more   _____

Part 4

Vocabulary Review

This is a review of all the vocabulary words you have learned in Chapters 6-10. Match each word on the left with the definition on the right by putting the correct letter in the blank. Look back at the words in the chapters if you need help with any of the definitions.

Chapters 6-8

A.

1. drop	_____	a. not like
2. indecisive	_____	b. to hold close
3. shovel	_____	c. thinking only of yourself
4. funny	_____	d. answer
5. dislike	_____	e. let fall
6. quick	_____	f. wait for
7. selfish	_____	g. to show anger by being quiet
8. offend	_____	h. not sure
9. reply	_____	i. of great importance
10. expect	_____	j. something that makes you laugh
11. urgent	_____	k. in the direction of
12. hug	_____	l. to make angry, insult
13. bent	_____	m. object used for picking things up
14. toward	_____	n. curved over
15. sulk	_____	o. fast

B.

1. possible	_____	a. to use more than is needed
2. waist	_____	b. felt very cold
3. follow	_____	c. sound made in speaking
4. voice	_____	d. angry
5. furious	_____	e. object used for fixing hair
6. pale	_____	f. go after
7. pail	_____	g. able to happen
8. soft	_____	h. angry
9. waste	_____	i. middle part of the body
10. exclaim	_____	j. gentle, kind
11. lean	_____	k. light in color
12. career	_____	l. skilled job
13. mad	_____	m. a round container for holding things
14. brush	_____	n. to speak with excitement
15. froze	_____	o. to rest one thing against another

Chapters 8-10

A.

1. squeeze	_____	a. to turn red
2. abrupt	_____	b. meaning what you say
3. confuse	_____	c. something difficult to understand
4. blush	_____	d. to like or love
5. serious	_____	e. willing to do anything to get what you want
6. except	_____	f. mistake one thing for another
7. accept	_____	g. all but some
8. puzzle	_____	h. sudden
9. rumor	_____	i. take

10. relax	_____	j. to look sad
11. desperate	_____	k. beautiful
12. care	_____	l. aware, knowing about
13. frown	_____	m. press on both sides
14. lovely	_____	n. rest
15. conscious	_____	o. information that may not be true

B.

1. complicated	_____	a. meeting between a man and a woman
2. cry	_____	b. other, different
3. else	_____	c. take quickly
4. personal	_____	d. wanting to own or have power over
5. finally	_____	e. private
6. hardly	_____	f. having many parts
7. possessive	_____	g. to call out loudly
8. react	_____	h. toward the front
9. forward	_____	i. should
10. embarrass	_____	j. quiet, peaceful
11. date	_____	k. to feel nervous or silly
12. grab	_____	l. almost not at all
13. concern	_____	m. at last
14. ought	_____	n. troubled interest
15. calm	_____	o. to do something in answer to something else

Part 5

Idioms Review

This is a review of all the idioms you learned in Chapters 6-10. Match the part of the sentence on the left that goes together with the end of the sentence on the right by putting the correct letter in the blank.

Chapters 6-8

1. No one had television 60 years ago, but times . . . _____
2. When he found out he'd been robbed he was so mad . . . _____
3. No one else came to help me move, but at . . . _____
4. When I talk to you please pay . . . _____
5. There was such a mess after the party that they worked for hours to fix . . . _____
6. When she couldn't fix the lamp she had to give . . . _____
7. After their fight Gloria followed Bradley so she could make . . . _____
8. He put his arms around her as his lips . . . _____
9. When he heard Ellen behind him he turned . . . _____
10. The pain made his face turn . . . _____
11. After school please stop . . . _____
12. Pick up your sick child as . . . _____

a. soon as possible.
b. least Harry is here.
c. up and buy a new one.
d. met hers
e. around.
f. pale.
g. things up in the house.
h. he didn't know which way to go first.
i. have changed.
j. up with him.
k. attention.
l. by my house.

Chapters 8-10

1. The soup can't be done yet. It's only been cooking for a little . . . _____
2. I knew he was upset when he put his head . . . _____
3. I'm going to break up with Miguel. I don't want to . . . _____
4. Now that I've lived here for a month, I'm beginning to get . . . _____
5. If you thought it was too late to go, why didn't you say . . . _____
6. I didn't expect to run . . . _____
7. I know it's late, but so . . . _____
8. He asked her if she would go . . . _____
9. Please ask questions. Don't . . . _____
10. The story was so funny that she threw . . . _____
11. Beatrice said you needed me. What . . . _____

a. so?
b. hold back.
c. into Ivan at the party.
d. out with him.
e. is it?
f. back her head and laughed.
g. to know the city.
h. in his hands.
i. what? Let's go out anyway.
j. while.
k. see him anymore.

Chapter 11

Whose Side Are You On?

Chapter *11*

Whose Side Are You On?

Part 1

Vocabulary

These are the vocabulary words you will learn in this chapter. Each word has a definition and a sentence. Notice that many words have more than one meaning.

1. **annoy** (verb)—bother, make angry
   It annoys me when someone I hardly know asks personal questions.

2. **unusual** (adjective)—strange, not usual
   It's unusual for Rick to be late.

3. **couple** (noun)
   1) two of something
      Give me a couple of pieces of paper.
   2) a man and a woman who are married, dating, or dancing together
      Kim and Ileana make a nice couple.

4. **relationship** (noun)—the connection, or tie, between people or things
   The relationship she has with her second husband is better than what she had with her first husband.
   There is a direct relationship between how much you eat and how much you weigh.

5. **stubborn** (adjective)
   1) not willing to change or do what someone else wants
      The stubborn boy wouldn't eat his peas even after his mother told him he couldn't have dessert.

147

2) difficult to move or treat
I've tried everything, but this stubborn cold just doesn't get any better.

6. **replace** (verb)
   1) to put something instead of (or in place of) something or someone else
   George Bush replaced Ronald Reagan as president.
   When our washing machine broke, we had to replace it with a new one.
   2) to put something back in its place
   Please replace the ladder after you've finished using it.

7. **lousy** (adjective) — bad
   I didn't like the movie. I thought it was lousy.

8. **defend** (verb)
   1) to fight for, protect
   We have an army to defend our country.
   2) to fight for in words, to write or speak in order to help someone
   When I heard the terrible rumors about my friend, I tried to defend her to the rest of the school.

9. **cafeteria** (noun) — a place to eat where you get food at a counter and carry it to the table yourself
   We always eat in the school cafeteria.

10. **realistic** (adjective)
    1) seeing things the way they really are, practical
    Because I didn't have much money, it was more realistic for me to buy a bicycle than to buy a car.
    2) something that looks like the real thing
    This movie is a realistic look at what life is like in Boston.

11. **enjoy** (verb) — like, have fun
    Frances enjoys her trip to Florida every year.

12. **act**
    1) (verb)—to be a certain way, behave
       He acted nervous because he knew the police were watching
          him.
    2) (verb)—to do something; (noun)—something done
       Thinking about going to school won't get you anywhere if you
          don't act on it.
       The soldier received many awards for his brave acts.
    3) (noun)—law
       Only an act of Congress could make that kind of change.
    4) (verb)—to take a part in a play, show, or movie, to perform;
      (noun)—a show or performance
       I always wanted to act in a play.
       The clown's act was very funny.
    5) (noun)—part of a play
       I thought the first act of the play was lovely, didn't you?

Idioms

Idioms are words that have special meanings in English when used together.

1. **run out on**—leave
   Her husband ran out on her.

2. **never mind**—forget it
   I called you to look at the funny TV commercial, but now it's gone.
     Never mind.

3. **ever since**—since then
   Carlos and Angela met on a blind date, and they've been together
     ever since.

4. **whose side are you on?**—which person or group do you agree with or defend?
   When the workers were on strike against the owner of the factory,
     they would ask the people in the town, "Whose side are you on?"

5. **Oh no!**—an exclamation you say when something bad has happened
   Oh no! There's water all over the floor!

Part 2

Vocabulary

Complete each of the following sentences with one of the vocabulary words on the list. Don't forget to read the words before the blank *and* the words after the blank to help you find the missing vocabulary word.

Remember that all of the answers (a, b, c) under one number are different meanings of the same word. When a word has more than one meaning, there is a parenthesis ( ) after the sentence. In the parenthesis put the number of the meaning from the vocabulary list in Part 1.

replace	stubborn
couple	enjoy
defend	relationship
realistic	cafeteria
act	lousy
annoy	unusual

1. a) In an emergency you must _____ quickly. ( )

   b) She always _____ (s) shy in front of her mother-in-law. ( )

   c) The actor is going to _____ in a new movie. ( )

   d) That law is an _____ of Congress. ( )

   e) We are watching a play in three _____ (s). ( )

2. a) It's only been a _____ of days since I've seen her. ( )

   b) A double date is a date for two _____ (s). ( )

3. When I want something quick to eat, I go to the _____ near my house.

4. We thought it was very _____ when it snowed in June.

5. a) When the children started to hit his sister, the boy went over to _____ her. ( )

b) If you go to court, you need a lawyer to _____ you. ( )

6. a) He wouldn't change his mind because he's very _____.

( )

b) This _____ door will not open. ( )

7. I don't want to go out because the weather is _____.

8. a) If you use one of the dictionaries, please _____ it when

you're finished. ( )

b) The brakes were bad in my car so I had to _____

them. ( )

9. He has a close _____ with his mother.

10. a) You have to be _____ about your chances of winning the

lottery. ( )

b) The movie *The Killing Fields* is a _____ story about

what life was really like in Cambodia. ( )

11. I _____ going to the movies, so I go every week.

12. It always _____ (s) me when a mosquito buzzes around my

head.

Idioms

Complete each of the following sentences with one of the idioms on the
list. Don't forget to read the words before the blank *and* the words after the blank to help you find the missing idioms.

    Oh no!
    ever since
    never mind
    run out on
    whose side are you on?

1. I fell and hit my leg and it's been hurting _____.

2. It's not important. _____ .

3. Don't _____ me when I need your help.

4. I thought you were my friend, yet you defend her and attack

   me. _____

5. _____ I've lost all my money!

Part 3

Summary

Bradley has left Samantha for Gloria. Samantha goes out with John Paul. When David and Jasmine tell her John Paul is seeing another woman, she asks him if it's true.

Questions to think and talk about before you read:

- Should Samantha keep seeing John Paul?
- What do you think Jasmine and David will think?

Episode 11. Whose Side Are You On?

A couple of days later at lunch, Samantha told Jasmine and David all about what she and John Paul had said in the bar.

"He didn't think there was anything unusual about seeing someone else and seeing me," said Samantha. "I couldn't believe it!"

"Well," said Jasmine, "he *was* going out with her before you met him on the beach that day. He had only known you a few days. What did you expect him to do?"

David looked angrily at Jasmine. "Whose side are you on? Why are you defending John Paul?"

"I have to say what I think," said Jasmine stubbornly. "I know you're feeling lousy, Samantha, but I think the real problem is that you're trying to replace Bradley with John Paul. You're trying to jump from one serious relationship into another, and it's just not realistic. You should just relax and enjoy yourself."

"Enjoy herself!" cried David. "What about all the things he said to her! What about the way he acted like he really cared about her!"

"What about the way he kissed me!" said Samantha. "And the way he touched me and . . ." She stopped abruptly and turned red with embarrassment. "Never mind," she continued. "The thing is that I've been so worried about the whole thing that I've been sick to my stomach."

"When did that start?" asked Jasmine, surprised.

"Right when I left the bar. And it's been bothering me ever since. I know I'm just nervous, but it really annoys me. Oh look, there he is!"

They all turned around to look as John Paul walked into the cafeteria.

"Oh, no!" said Samantha. "What should I do? He's walking this way!"

"You're not going to talk to him, are you?" exclaimed David.

"Why shouldn't she?" asked Jasmine.

Samantha sat frozen as John Paul walked over to their table and said, "Hi! Why did you run out on me the other night?"

Everyone stared at Samantha. Samantha looked down at the table and then up at John Paul. "Oh," she said, "I just wasn't feeling very well. Why don't you sit down, John Paul?"

Part 4

Questions

1. Whom is Samantha talking to?
2. Does Jasmine think John Paul is wrong?
3. What does Jasmine think the problem is between Samantha and John Paul? What does she think Samantha should do? Do you agree?
4. Does David agree with Jasmine?
5. What is Samantha talking about when she gets embarrassed?
6. What else has been annoying Samantha? Why does she think she's having this problem?
7. When John Paul walks into the cafeteria, does David think Samantha should talk to him?

8. Does Jasmine think Samantha should talk to John Paul?
9. Does Samantha talk to John Paul? What does she say is the reason she left the bar? Is that the only reason?
10. Do you think Samantha did the right thing in talking to John Paul? Why or why not?

Part 5

Fill in the blanks with your vocabulary words.

1. When you have a great time at a party, you _____ it.

2. When you want what you want, and nobody can change your mind, you feel _____ .

3. When people bother you, they _____ you.

4. Something you do that's strange is _____ .

5. The way you do something is the way you _____ .

6. When you have the flu, you feel _____ .

7. When you eat at a restaurant where you serve yourself, you are in a _____ .

8. When you give up plans to make money on the lottery and get a job instead, you are being _____ .

9. A man and a woman who get engaged are a _____ .

10. When something is broken, you _____ it with another one.

11. When someone attacks you, you _____ yourself.

12. When you have a good friend, you have a good _____ .

Part 6

There are eight vocabulary words spelled incorrectly in this copy of the story. Find the mistakes and correct them. The first one has been done for you.

A couple of days later at lunch, Samantha told Jasmine and David all about what she and John Paul had said in the bar.

"He didn't think there was anything unusual about seeing someone else and seeing me," said Samantha. "I couldn't believe it!"

"Well," said Jasmine, "he *was* going out with her before you met him on the beach that day. He had only known you a few days. What did you expect him to do?"

David looked angrily at Jasmine. "Whose side are you on? Why are you defending John Paul?"

"I have to say what I think," said Jasmine ~~stubornly~~ stubbornly. "I know you're feeling luosy, Samantha, but I think the real problem is that you're trying to riplace Bradley with John Paul. You're trying to jump from one serious relatonship to another, and it's just not realestec. You should just relax and engoy yourself."

"Enjoy herself!" cried David. "What about all the things he said to her! What about the way he acted like he really cared about her!"

"What about the way he kissed me!" said Samantha. "And the way he touched me and . . ." She stopped abruptly and turned red with embarrassment. "Never mind," she continued. "The thing is that I've been so worried about the whole thing that I've been sick to my stomach."

"When did that start?" asked Jasmine, surprised.

"Right when I left the bar. And it's been bothering me ever since. I know I'm just nervous, but it really anoys me. Oh look, there he is!"

They all turned around to look as John Paul walked into the cafateria.

"Oh no!" said Samantha. "What should I do? He's walking this way!"

"You're not going to talk to him, are you?" exclaimed David.

"Why shouldn't she?" asked Jasmine.

Samantha sat frozen as John Paul walked over to their table and said, "Hi! Why did you run out on me the other night?"

Everyone stared at Samantha. Samantha looked down at the table and then up at John Paul. "Oh," she said, "I just wasn't feeling very well. Why don't you sit down, John Paul?"

Chapter 12
Oh No!

Chapter *12*

Oh No!

Part 1

Vocabulary

These are the vocabulary words you will learn in this chapter. Each word has a definition and a sentence. Notice that many words have more than one meaning.

1. **frighten** (verb)—to be scared or afraid; **frightened** (adjective)—scared or afraid
   Kittens frighten easily.
   The frightened girl squeezed her mother's hand.

2. **pensive** (adjective)—thinking, thoughtful
   The character in the movie had a pensive look on his face.

3. **improve** (verb)—to get better
   I hope the weather will improve so we can go on the picnic.

4. **ignore** (verb)—pay no attention to
   When her boyfriend became jealous and possessive, she just ignored him.
   It may be easy to ignore your problems, but they won't go away.

5. **examination** (noun)
   1) looking at something carefully, investigation
      He made a complete examination of the table before he decided to buy it.

2) looking at the body carefully, by a doctor or other medical worker
When the woman became conscious after the operation, the doctor came in to do an examination.

3) a test of what you know
At the end of each chapter, the teacher will give an examination.

6. **result** (noun)—something that happens because of something else; (verb)—to happen because of something else
He went to the hospital to get the results of his examination.
Mary's talk with the boss resulted in her getting fired.

7. **interrupt** (verb)
1) to speak when someone else is already talking
I can't finish my story if you keep interrupting me.

2) to stop for a time and then continue
We interrupt this TV program for a short message from the president.

8. **fact** (noun)—something true, something that has happened
It's a fact that Abraham Lincoln was the 16th president of the United States.
Check your facts to be sure they are true.

9. **recognize** (verb)
1) to know again
I hadn't been to San Francisco in so many years that I didn't recognize it.

2) to show you accept or approve
The teacher recognized Sarah's hard work by reading her story to the class.
A country will recognize another country if it approves of its government.

10. **realize** (verb)—to understand, know, especially something you didn't know before
I realize you're hungry, but dinner won't be ready for another half hour.

> *After I went to my first meeting of Alcoholics Anonymous, I realized that I, too, was an alcoholic.*

11. **consult** (verb) — to look for information or advice from
    Because she didn't know the answer to my question, Meryl had to consult another teacher.
    To find out the vocabulary words for this lesson, consult the list at the beginning of the chapter.

12. **preoccupied** (adjective) — deep in thought, especially while doing something else
    She was so preoccupied with her problems at work, that she burned the chicken she was cooking.

Idioms

Idioms are words that have special meaning in English when used together.

1. **give someone a checkup** — give someone an examination by a doctor or other medical worker
   Dr. Solomon is going to give Marsha a checkup.

2. **what's the matter?** — what's the problem?
   You look annoyed. What's the matter?

3. **drive someone crazy** — to bother or annoy someone
   He's going to drive me crazy if he doesn't stop playing that record over and over again.
   This cold is driving me crazy.

4. **get up** — stand up
   Karen got up and walked over to the window.

Part 2

Vocabulary

Complete each of the following sentences with one of the words on the list. Don't forget to read the words before the blank *and* the words after the blank to help you find the missing vocabulary word.

Remember that all the answers (a, b, c) under one number are different meanings of the same word. When a word has more than one meaning, there is a parenthesis ( ) after the sentence. In the parenthesis put the number of the meaning from the vocabulary list in Part 1.

recognize	consult
improve	fact
frighten	pensive
result	ignore
examination	preoccupied
realize	interrupt

1. It is a _____ that the world is round.

2. Her big bank account is the _____ of years of hard work.

3. If you continue to feel sick, you should _____ a doctor.

4. I hate it when you don't pay attention to me; don't _____ me.

5. If you want to _____ your reading, you should read more.

6. When he heard the noise of thunder, the little boy was

   _____ (ed).

7. a) Parents usually teach their children, "Wait until I'm finished! Don't _____ me when I'm talking." ( )

   b) His illness _____ (ed) his schooling. ( )

8. Cinderella suddenly _____ (d) that it was later than she thought. It was almost midnight!

9. a) She had lost weight and changed her hair, so when I saw her I didn't _____ her. ( )

   b) Because it did not approve of China's government, the U.S. did not _____ the Republic of China for many years. ( )

10. a) The doctor's _____ showed that George was perfectly

   healthy. ( )

   b) He is going to take the GED _____ . ( )

   c) The _____ of his records showed he had been stealing

   money from the company. ( )

11. You look very _____ ; what are you thinking about?

12. He was so _____ with thinking about his problem that he

   didn't hear a word I said.

Idioms

Complete each of the following sentences with one of the idioms on the
list. Don't forget to read the words before the blank *and* the words after
the blank to help you find the missing idiom.

   get up
   give me a checkup
   driving me crazy
   what's the matter?

1. Every time we go to the beach it rains. This lousy weather is

   _____ .

2. I asked my doctor to _____ .

3. I heard you went to the hospital today. _____

4. I want you all to _____ from your chairs and

   walk quietly to the door.

Part 3

Summary

Bradley has left Samantha for Gloria. Samantha meets and goes out
with John Paul. Her friends Jasmine and David tell her John Paul is
seeing another woman.

Questions to think and talk about before you read:

- Do you think Samantha will be happy now going out with John Paul?
- What do you think could be wrong with Samantha's stomach?

Episode 12. Oh No!

Samantha continued to go out with John Paul. She tried to ignore the fact that he was going out with someone else. She didn't think about Bradley so much anymore and thought instead about making a new life for herself without Bradley. Her life was starting to improve.

The only problem she still had was that her stomach continued to bother her. Finally, she decided it was time to consult a doctor about it.

"John Paul," she said one day as they were eating dinner, "I don't have a regular doctor. Could you give me a checkup? My stomach is driving me crazy."

"Sure," he said. "Come and see me at the hospital tomorrow when you finish work, and I'll examine you and do some tests."

Two days later Samantha went to John Paul's office to get the results of the examination and the tests he had done on her. When she entered the office and saw his face she became very frightened. He looked so serious, so preoccupied. Nervously she sat down next to his desk.

"What's the matter?" she asked with concern. "Am I very sick? Am I going to die?"

John Paul got up from his desk and walked across the room. Then he turned around and looked at her pensively.

"Tell me! Tell me!"

He walked over to the desk and looked at her again. "You're pregnant," he said sadly.

"What!?" exclaimed Samantha. "Are you sure?"

"Very sure," he answered. "I waited to tell you until I was quite sure."

"But you ... but you and I ..."

"Samantha," he interrupted, "you're at least eight weeks pregnant."

Samantha thought back to the weeks before she knew John Paul, and then she realized what she had not wanted to recognize before.

"Oh no!" she said. "It's Bradley's!"

Part 4

Questions

1. Does Samantha continue to go out with John Paul?
2. How does Samantha feel about her life?
3. What is her only problem?
4. What does she ask John Paul to do?
5. Why does Samantha go to John Paul's office two days later?
6. What does she see in John Paul's face that frightens her?
7. What is she frightened of?
8. What is wrong with Samantha?
9. What does Samantha realize when she says, "Oh no!"
10. How does she know that it's Bradley's?

Part 5

Fill in the blanks with words from the vocabulary list. On the left are the letters of the word you need, but the letters are not in the correct order.

1. enepisv — thinking   _____

2. ecorpecuipd — thinking about one thing while doing

   something else   _____

3. tniuretrp — to stop in the middle   _____

4. actf — something true   _____

5. igconerze — to see something you've seen before   _____

6. uocnstl — to go for information or advice   _____

7. evrmipo — to get better   _____

8. eoginr — to not pay attention   _____

9. ezlerai — to think of something you haven't

   thought of before   _____

10. oimeaxanitn — looking at something very

    carefully   _____

11. enegrfihtd — scared   _____

12. tesurl — when you cause something to happen

    you get this   _____

Part 6

There are eight vocabulary words spelled incorrectly in this copy of the story. Find the mistakes and correct them. The first one has been done for you.

      Samantha continued to go out with John Paul. She tried to

ignore

~~ignure~~ the fact that he was going out with someone else. She didn't

think about Bradley so much anymore and thought instead about mak-

ing a new life for herself without Bradley. Her life was starting to

improve.

      The only problem she still had was that her stomach continued

to bother her. Finally, she decided it was time to cunsult a doctor

about it.

      "John Paul," she said one day as they were eating dinner, "I

don't have a regular doctor. Could you give me a checkup? My stomach

is driving me crazy."

      "Sure," he said. "Come and see me at the hospital tomorrow

when you finish work, and I'll examine you and do some tests."

Two days later Samantha went to John Paul's office to get the results of the exeminaciun and the tests he had done on her. When she entered the office and saw his face she became very frihgtened. He looked so serious, so preocupied. Nervously she sat down next to his desk.

"What's the matter?" she asked with concern. "Am I very sick? Am I going to die?"

John Paul got up from his desk and walked across the room. Then he turned around and looked at her pensively.

"Tell me! Tell me!"

He walked over to the desk and looked at her again. "You're pregnant," he said sadly.

"What!?" exclaimed Samantha. "Are you sure?"

"Very sure," he answered. "I waited to tell you until I was quite sure."

"But you . . . but you and I . . ."

"Samantha," he interupted, "you're at least eight weeks pregnant."

Samantha thought back to the weeks before she knew John Paul, and then she realised what she had not wanted to recognise before.

"Oh no!" she said. "It's Bradley's!"

Chapter 13

Talking Things Over

Chapter *13*

Talking Things Over

Part 1

Vocabulary

These are the vocabulary words you will learn in this chapter. Each word has a definition and a sentence. Notice that many words have more than one meaning.

1. **infant** (noun) — baby
   The infant was taken to the doctor for her first examination.

2. **miserable** (adjective); **miserably** (adverb)
   1) very unhappy
      Rachel's cold is making her miserable.
      "I have no money and I just lost my job," Vinh said miserably.
   2) causing sadness; bad
      This miserable weather is making me depressed.
      I'm very upset about the miserable job you did.
      I did miserably on the test.

3. **rush** (verb) — to hurry, move or act quickly; (adjective) — hurried; (noun) — quick movement
   The police rushed to the bank where the robbers were hiding.
   Rush hour is the time when people hurry home from work.
   He was late so he was in a rush.
   When they opened the doors a rush of people entered the theater.

4. **discuss** (verb) — to talk or write about
   I don't want to discuss this in front of the children.
   *This magazine discusses some of the common ideas people have
      about marriage.*

5. **adoption** (noun)
   1) legally taking another person's child for your own
      The woman was too poor and sick to take care of her baby, so she gave the child up for adoption. [see Idioms, #1.]
   2) agreement to use as your own
      They believed that adoption of a new Constitution would improve the government.

6. **option** (noun)—choice, power to decide between more than one thing
   I suddenly realized that I was in danger and I had no other option than to get out of there fast!

7. **abortion** (noun)—operation to end a pregnancy before the normal time of birth
   She didn't want to have an abortion, and she couldn't keep the baby, so she gave it up for adoption.

8. **shock**
   1) (noun)—an upsetting surprise; (verb)—to surprise in an upsetting way
      Finding out her son had run away and got married was a shock to Angela.
      Samantha was shocked when she found out she was pregnant.
   2) (noun)—the feeling of electricity going through a person's body
      The little boy got a shock when he touched the electrical plug.
   3) (noun)—a serious reaction to being hurt, when the workings of the body slow down
      The doctor saw that the bleeding man was in shock.

9. **tissue** (noun)—a very thin paper used to clean the nose and then thrown away, paper handkerchief; tissue paper is a thin paper used for wrapping
   The man blew his nose into a tissue.
   He wrapped the glass in tissue paper so it wouldn't break.

10. **support**
    1) (verb)—to give money or other needed things; (noun)—needs
       My parents are going to help support me while I go to school.
       Her ex-husband gives her money for the children's support.

2) (verb)—to hold up and keep from falling; (noun)—something that holds things up
   These pieces of wood support the roof.
   Some of the supports for the bridge are broken, so it's dangerous to use.

3) (verb)—to be on the side of, encourage, help; (noun)—the act of being on the side of, encouragement, help
   Who do you support for mayor?
   Her belief in God supports her in times of trouble.
   I give my support to the Red Sox.

4) (verb)—to give facts for, help prove
   These facts support the results of the doctor's medical study.

11. wipe

1) (verb)—rub or take off to make dry or clean; (noun)—a rub to make dry or clean
   Mary Ellen wiped off the car window so she could see out.
   The little boy tried to wipe the tears off his sister's face.
   Michael gave the table a wipe with the sponge.

2) wipe out—to destroy or kill
   The storm wiped out the whole town.

12. otherwise (adverb)

1) in another way, differently
   She ran out of the movie theater. The movie frightened her so much that she could not do otherwise.

2) if not, except for that
   Study, otherwise you won't pass the test.
   You learn things in school that you might not know otherwise.

Idioms

Idioms are words that have special meanings in English when used together.

1. give the child up—give the child to someone else
   My ex-husband wants my daughter to live with him, but I won't give the child up.
   They gave the child up for adoption.

2. **go on**—continue

   It's not realistic for me to go on working at three jobs; I'm too tired.

3. **go back**—return, go where you were before

   The break is over. We have to go back to class now.

4. **come over**—come for a visit; **come right over**—come for a visit at once, quickly

   Why don't you come over to my house after work?

   Come right over; we're eating dinner in fifteen minutes.

Part 2

Vocabulary

Complete each of the following sentences. Don't forget to read the words before the blank *and* the words after the blank to help you find the missing vocabulary word.

   Remember that all the answers (a, b, c) under one number are different meanings of the same word. When a word has more than one meaning, there is a parenthesis ( ) after the sentence. In the parenthesis put the number of the meaning from the vocabulary list in Part I.

abortion	support
infant	miserable
wipe	rush
adoption	discuss
option	shock
otherwise	tissue

1. a) He was so heavy that the chair could not _____ his

   weight, so it broke. ( )

   b) Her job does not give her enough money to _____ her

   family. ( )

c) He gave a lot of information to ＿＿＿＿＿＿ his idea. ( )

d) Her friends gave her a lot of ＿＿＿＿＿＿ after the

operation. ( )

2. a) When the wire touched the water, Pierre got an electrical

＿＿＿＿＿＿ . ( )

b) It was a ＿＿＿＿＿＿ when she found out that her father was

in the hospital. ( )

c) After the car accident, the woman went into ＿＿＿＿＿＿ . ( )

3. The ＿＿＿＿＿＿ in the baby carriage is only three months old.

4. a) She lives in a ＿＿＿＿＿＿ little room, in an old building, in a

lousy neighborhood. ( )

b) When the couple broke up, they both felt ＿＿＿＿＿＿ . ( )

5. a) If you want children and cannot have them yourself, you might

want to think about ＿＿＿＿＿＿ . ( )

b) The ＿＿＿＿＿＿ of some unusual ideas saved the company a

lot of money. ( )

6. a) You wash the dishes and I'll ＿＿＿＿＿＿ them with this

towel. ( )

b) The killer planned to ＿＿＿＿＿＿ out the man he hated. ( )

7. The ambulance ＿＿＿＿＿＿ (ed) to the accident.

8. When Debora saw Tatia crying, she handed her a ＿＿＿＿＿＿ .

9. You have two ＿＿＿＿＿＿ (s); you can go by car or by bus.

10. I decided to ＿＿＿＿＿＿ the problem with my teacher to see if

she could help.

11. An operation to end a pregnancy is called an ＿＿＿＿＿＿ .

12. a) Take your umbrella, _____ you will get wet. ( )

b) She smiled. She was so happy to see him she could not behave

_____ . ( )

Idioms

Complete each of the following sentences with one of the idioms on the list. Don't forget to read the words before the blank *and* the words after the blank to help you find the missing idiom.

> gave the child up
> go on
> came right over
> go back

1. When Helen heard I was in trouble, she _____ .

2. After living in the U.S. for a year, Miguel decided to

_____ to El Salvador.

3. After little Lisa's parents died, her grandmother was too old to take

care of her, so she _____ for adoption.

4. Now that Les and I have broken up, I have to forget about romance

and _____ with my life.

Part 3

Summary

Bradley has left Samantha for Gloria. Samantha is going out with John Paul when she finds out she is pregnant and the father is her husband Bradley.

Questions to think and talk about before you read:

- What do you think Samantha will do now?
- Do you think she'll go back to Bradley?

Episode 13. Talking Things Over

After John Paul gave her the news that she was pregnant, Saman- tha just sat in his office for a minute in shock. Then she said nervously, "I have to go home and think, John Paul," and rushed out.

As she drove home she was so preoccupied with thoughts about her pregnancy that she was afraid she was going to have an accident. "What am I going to do?" she thought. "My life was just beginning to be a little normal, and now this!"

As soon as she arrived home, she called Jasmine and told her what happened. Jasmine came right over to Samantha's house.

"What am I going to do?" asked Samantha, starting to wipe her eyes with a tissue. "How can I have a baby now?"

"Well," said Jasmine, "do you want to have a baby?"

"Maybe someday, but not now," answered Samantha. "I'm alone. Bradley's with Gloria! How can I support an infant?"

"You could go back to Bradley," answered Jasmine.

"Go back! After the way he acted!" said Samantha angrily.

"Well, he *is* the father. Are you going to tell him?"

"I don't know," said Samantha, starting to cry. "I wish the whole thing would just go away!"

"That's another option you have," said Jasmine quietly. "You could make it go away."

Samantha stopped crying. "You mean have an abortion, or give the child up for adoption? Oh, I don't know if I could."

"That's the only way your life could go on as it was," Jasmine continued, "working at the hospital and going out with John Paul. Oth- erwise, everything will change."

"Oh, John Paul!" answered Samantha miserably. "What about him? I didn't even discuss it with him." She thought for a minute. "Maybe he would marry me."

"Do you *want* to marry him?"

"Well, I'd rather be married to him than to Bradley, I guess," answered Samantha pensively, "although right now I'm not sure I want to be married to anyone."

Jasmine walked over to Samantha and hugged her. "It's a difficult decision," she said, "but I'll support you any way I can."

Part 4

Questions

1. How does Samantha feel after John Paul tells her she's pregnant?
2. Whom does she call when she get home?
3. Does Samantha want to have a baby now?
4. What is the first idea Jasmine gives?
5. Does Samantha want to go back with Bradley? Why or why not?
6. How does Samantha feel about having an abortion or giving the child up for adoption?
7. Does it sound like she really wants to marry John Paul?
8. Does Samantha want to be married?
9. What kind of friend is Jasmine being to Samantha?
10. What do you think would be the best thing for Samantha to do?

Part 5

Look back at the word list to help you find and circle the twelve vocabulary words in the puzzle. The words can be spelled forward or backward, and in any direction. There are also two extra words from the story, *accident* and *afraid.* See if you can find all fourteen words. One word has been done for you.

```
S  A  L  H  E  C  K  A  R  A  H  A  R  B  R  N
P  B  E  M  P  A  O  T  H  E  R  W  I  S  E  A
E  C  F  E  B  B  P  N  V  E  U  S  S  I  T  C
H  D  O  N  P  O  T  A  W  R  O  I  E  R  H  C
D  T  P  B  E  R  I  D  N  I  N  G  T  S  G  I
D  N  N  A  I  T  O  O  S  B  P  G  B  L  U  D
H  I  T  A  S  I  N  P  Q  M  V  E  M  R  O  E
J  F  A  M  F  O  W  T  P  R  M  T  P  T  H  N
L  G  C  R  D  N  P  I  S  U  P  P  O  R  T  T
P  O  R  E  F  W  I  O  M  S  D  E  F  T  P  N
W  U  T  S  S  A  S  N  S  H  O  C  K  E  I  O
D  I  S  C  U  S  S  E  L  B  A  R  E  S  I  M
```

Part 6

There are nine vocabulary words spelled incorrectly in this copy of the story, and one word has been spelled wrong two times. Notice the *two different uses* of that word. Find the mistakes and correct them. The first one has been done for you.

After John Paul gave her the news that she was pregnant, Samantha just sat in his office for a minute in ~~shok~~ shock. Then she said nervously, "I have to go home and think, John Paul," and rushed out.

As she drove home she was so preoccupied with thoughts about her pregnancy that she was afraid she was going to have an accident. "What am I going to do?" she thought. "My life was just beginning to be a little more normal, and now this!"

As soon as she arrived home, she called Jasmine and told her what happened. Jasmine came right over to Samantha's house.

"What am I going to do?" asked Samantha, starting to whipe her eyes with a tisue. "How can I have a baby now?"

"Well," said Jasmine, "do you want to have a baby?"

"Maybe someday, but not now," answered Samantha. "I'm alone. Bradley's with Gloria! How can I sepport an infent?"

"You could go back to Bradley," answered Jasmine.

"Go back! After the way he acted!" said Samantha angrily.

"Well, he *is* the father. Are you going to tell him?"

"I don't know," said Samantha, starting to cry. "I wish the whole thing would just go away!"

"That's another opion you have," said Jasmine quietly. "You could make it go away."

Samantha stopped crying. "You mean have an abortion, or give the child up for adoption? Oh, I don't know if I could."

"That's the only way your life could go on as it was," Jasmine continued, "working at the hospital and going out with John Paul. Otherwice, everything will change."

"Oh, John Paul!" answered Samantha miserably. "What about him? I didn't even discus it with him." She thought for a minute. "Maybe he would marry me."

"Do you *want* to marry him?"

"Well, I'd rather be married to him than to Bradley, I guess," answered Samantha pensively, "although right now I'm not sure I want to be married to anyone."

Jasmine walked over to Samantha and hugged her. "It's a difficult decision," she said, "but I'll suport you any way I can."

Chapter 14

A Nice Guy?

A Nice Guy?

Part 1

Vocabulary

These are the vocabulary words you will learn in this chapter. Each word has a definition and a sentence. Notice that many words have more than one meaning.

1. **guy** (noun)—boy or man
   It is often the custom for two guys who are friends to arrange a double date.

2. **uncomfortable** (adjective)
   1) not relaxed and easy in your body
      The heat in this room is making me uncomfortable.
   2) not relaxed and easy in your mind
      I was confused and uncomfortable when I suddenly realized everyone was staring at me.

3. **oversleep** (verb) (past tense—**overslept**)—to sleep longer than you should
   I'll call you at 7 A.M. so you don't oversleep.
   Wendy almost missed her appointment because she overslept.

4. **anxious**
   1) (adjective)—worried, nervous; **anxiously** (adverb)—in a worried or nervous manner
      He felt anxious about his sick child.
      "Is it dangerous for a week-old infant to have such a high fever?" she asked anxiously.

2) (adjective)—excited, wanting very much to do something
   Robert was anxious to try out his exciting new career.

5. **dawn**
   1) (noun)—the time when the sun comes up and it gets light;
      (verb)—to begin to get light in the morning
      Steve had to get up at dawn to get ready for the trip.
      The day dawned beautiful and sunny.
   2) (noun)—the beginning of something; (verb)—to begin something
      I've gone back to school; it's the dawn of a new time for me.
      The first airplane flight was the dawning of a new age in
         America.
   3) (verb)—to realize
      When she hadn't seen Felix in a month, it finally dawned on her
         that their relationship was in trouble.

6. **restless** (adjective)—not able to rest or sleep, not able to relax or
   stay quiet
   When her child was sick, Ruth had a restless night.
   I was too restless to sit in the house, so I went for a walk.

7. **entangle** (verb); **entangled** (adjective)
   1) to get mixed together and caught, for example, string, thread,
      etc.
      The rope was entangled in the fence.
      The kite string became entangled in a tree and we couldn't get
         it down.
   2) to get caught in something difficult, involved in trouble
      Don't entangle me in your plans to rob the store.
      He became entangled in his own lies until everyone recognized
         he wasn't telling the truth.

8. **affect** (verb)
   1) to cause a result or change on something
      Sun and rain affect the growth of plants.
   2) to cause an emotional feeling
      The sad story of the homeless woman affected Morris so much
         that he gave her all the money in his wallet.

9. **disturb**
   1) (verb)—to mix up, move out of place
      Please don't disturb the papers on the desk.
   2) (verb)—to bother, interrupt, upset; **disturbed** (adjective)—upset, bothered
      Do not disturb Mother when she's sleeping.
      He was disturbed to hear the bad news.

10. **bitter**
    1) (adjective)—having a bad, sour taste
       This coffee has been on the stove too long; it tastes bitter.
    2) (adjective); **bitterly** (adverb)—angry in a cold way, resentful
       The two men hated each other. They'd been bitter enemies for years.
       He looked bitterly at his ex-wife and tried to ignore her when she spoke to him.
    3) (adjective)—very cold
       The bitter wind blew through the house.

11. **hesitate** (verb)—to stop for a short time, or be slow to act or speak because you're afraid or not sure
    The student hesitated before answering the difficult question.
    If you hesitate too long, all the tickets will be gone.

12. **earnest** (adjective)—sincere, showing you mean what you say or do; **earnestly** (adverb)—in a sincere way
    Alejandro made an earnest try to defend his sister against the older boys, but they were too big for him.
    This school is full of earnest students.
    "Please don't be so stubborn; let me help you!" she said earnestly.

Idioms

Idioms are words that have special meanings in English when used together.

1. **what difference does it make?** — an expression showing that it doesn't matter, it doesn't cause a problem
   If Don doesn't come today, he can come tomorrow. What difference does it make?

2. **no matter what** — without caring or concern for
   No matter what school you choose, you'll learn more than you know now.

3. **fall asleep** — to go to sleep
   The little girl tried not to fall asleep, but we could see her eyes closing.
   John fell asleep while watching "Star Trek" on TV.

4. **up to you** (him, her, me, them) — it's your (his, her, my, their) choice or decision
   "If you want to consult another doctor, that's up to you," said Dr. Sherman.
   Mother said the decision was up to me.

5. **stop in** — stop by, go to see for a short time
   Debbie is going to stop in to see Lennie after the meeting.

6. **have nothing to do with me** (him, her, you) — it's not connected to me (him, her, you); it's not my (his, her, your) problem
   If you spilled the milk, you have to wipe it up. It has nothing to do with me.
   Don't worry, what we're discussing has nothing to do with you.

7. **even if** — although
   This will taste good even if we eat it cold.

8. **of course** — certainly, for sure
   Do you love me? Of course I do.

9. **as long as** — only if
   I won't worry as long as I know you're with your older brother.

Part 2

Vocabulary

Complete each of the following sentences with one of the words on the list. Don't forget to read the words before the blank *and* the words after the blank to help you find the missing vocabulary words.

Remember that all the answers (a, b, c) under one number are different meanings of the same word. When a word has more than one meaning, there is a parenthesis ( ) after the sentence. In the parenthesis put the number of the meaning from the vocabulary list in Part 1.

earnest	uncomfortable
bitter	hesitate
guy	affect
dawn	disturb
restless	anxious
oversleep	entangle

1. a) I love to watch the sunrise; I think _____ is the most beautiful time of the day. ( )

   b) After waiting for an hour, it _____ (ed) on him that she wasn't coming. ( )

   c) Now that I've stopped using drugs, a new life is _____ (ing) for me. ( )

2. When my alarm clock doesn't ring, I _____ .

3. The _____ over there looking at the advertisement is my brother.

4. She was so _____ that she couldn't sit still.

5. She didn't know whether to interrupt him or not, so she _____ (d) at the door.

6. a) Bad weather _____ (s) school attendance. ( )

   b) She was so _____ (ed) by the sad movie that she started to cry. ( )

7. a) Don't _____ Amalia. She's studying. ( )

   b) If Susie doesn't want the baby to _____ her Barbie dolls, she should put them on a high shelf. ( )

8. a) While she waited for the doctor's report, she felt

      _____ . ( )

   b) Hal was _____ to try out his new car. ( )

9. Heng's _____ face showed he meant every word he said.

10. a) She always got her family _____ (d) in her fights with her husband. ( )

    b) The kitten became _____ (d) in the string. ( )

11. a) He felt _____ after sitting in the hard chair for so long. ( )

    b) Because he was shy, he felt _____ at parties. ( )

12. a) Put on warm clothes; it's _____ outside. ( )

    b) He felt _____ about the hard life he had had. ( )

    c) A lemon tastes _____ . ( )

Idioms

Complete each of the following sentences with one of the idioms on the list. Don't forget to read the words before the blank *and* the words after the blank to help you with the missing idioms.

fall asleep
what difference does it make?
no matter what
nothing to do with her
even if

up to him
of course
as long as
stop in

1. I plan to continue with the adoption _____ it

   costs me.

2. I couldn't _____ because I drank too much

   coffee.

3. He doesn't have to come if he doesn't want to. It's _____ .

4. In this recipe I'm sure you can use margarine instead of butter.

   _____

5. This problem is not Terry's fault. It has _____ .

6. Do I want some ice cream? _____ .

7. Let's _____ to see Mohammed.

8. You can go out _____ you're home early.

9. Don't worry, _____ the train is late, we'll still

   get there on time.

Part 3

Summary

Bradley has left Samantha for Gloria. Samantha is going out with John Paul when she finds out she is pregnant and the father is her husband Bradley. She talks to Jasmine about it.

Questions to think and talk about before you read:

- What do you think John Paul will say about Samantha's pregnancy?
- Do you think he will want to marry her?

Episode 14. A Nice Guy?

After Jasmine left, Samantha had a restless night. She finally fell asleep at dawn and overslept. Although she was late to work, she took the time to stop in at John Paul's office and ask him to have dinner with her so that they could talk. John Paul hesitated, and then agreed to see her that night.

They chose a quiet restaurant where they could talk. "Well," Samantha said, leaning back in her chair, "you know my problem. What do you think I should do?"

"That's not for me to decide," answered John Paul quietly. "You're the one who has to make the decision."

"Of course," said Samantha, trying to smile, "but I could use some help."

"I always try to keep out of other people's problems, especially the women I go out with."

"But you're the man I'm dating," answered Samantha, beginning to get disturbed. "What I do affects you. What if I decide to have the baby?"

"If you have the baby, that's up to you," said John Paul, buttering a piece of bread. "It has nothing to do with me."

"But if I have the baby, I'll need the support of my friends and the people who care about me," answered Samantha anxiously.

"Please understand me," said John Paul, putting down the bread and staring at her earnestly. "I would enjoy seeing you, no matter what option you choose. Even if you had the baby, we could still have a good time together—when you had time. I just don't like to get entangled in my women's problems. Your life is your own."

Now Samantha was beginning to get angry. "You don't care what happens to me," she said angrily, "as long as you keep on having a good time. And what's all this you keep saying about 'your women'? How many women are you seeing anyway?"

For the first time John Paul began to look uncomfortable and a little nervous. He tried to put back his usual smile and took her hand. "What difference does it make how many women I see? You're here with me now, aren't you? We have fun together and we can keep on having fun."

Samantha stared at him.

"It would be a lot easier without the baby," he continued, relaxing, "but if you did have the baby it wouldn't have much effect on me. I would still see you." He laughed. "See what a nice guy I am?"

"Oh, you're a real nice guy," said Samantha bitterly. "A real nice guy."

Part 4

Questions

1. What did Samantha ask John Paul when she got to work?
2. Why do you think John Paul hesitated before answering her?
3. Does Samantha think the baby would affect John Paul?
4. Does John Paul think the baby would affect him? What does he say to show this?
5. John Paul says he doesn't want to get entangled in Samantha's problems. Do you agree?
6. Does John Paul seem to want to help Samantha? Why or why not?
7. When Samantha asks John Paul how many women he's seeing, does he answer her? How is he feeling?
8. What does John Paul want with Samantha? What does Samantha want?
9. Does Samantha think John Paul is a nice guy? Do you think he's a nice guy?

Part 5

Fill in the blanks with words from the vocabulary list.

1. A person who can't rest is _____.

2. When the sun comes up is _____.

3. When you don't wake up when you're supposed to, you

   _____ .

4. To stop and wait before continuing: _____

5. Another word for a man is _____ .

6. When you're worried about something about to happen:

   _____

7. When you're sincere; you really mean it: _____

8. When you get mixed up in something you don't want to be mixed

   up in: _____

9. When you're not relaxed in your body or mind: _____

10. When something tastes sour and bad: _____

11. To cause a change in something: _____

12. To bother or upset someone: _____

Part 6

There are nine vocabulary words spelled incorrectly in this copy of the story. Find the mistakes, and correct them. The first one has been done for you.

                                     restless
    After Jasmine left, Samantha had a ~~restles~~ night. She finally fell asleep at down and overslept. Although she was late to work, she took the time to stop in at John Paul's office and ask him to have dinner with her so that they could talk. John Paul hesatated, and then agreed to see her that night.

    They chose a quiet restaurant where they could talk. "Well," Samantha said, leaning back in her chair, "you know my problem. What do you think I should do?"

"That's not for me to decide," answered John Paul quietly. "You're the one who has to make the decision."

"Of course," said Samantha, trying to smile, "but I could use some help."

"I always try to keep out of other people's problems, especially the women I go out with."

"But you're the man I'm dating," answered Samantha, beginning to get disterbed. "What I do efects you. What if I decide to have the baby?"

"If you have the baby, that's up to you," said John Paul, buttering a piece of bread. "It has nothing to do with me."

"But if I have the baby, I'll need the support of my friends and the people who care about me," answered Samantha anxiosly.

"Please understand me," said John Paul, putting down the bread and staring at her ernestly. "I would enjoy seeing you, no matter what option you choose. Even if you had the baby, we could still have a good time together—when you had time. I just don't like to get entangeled in my women's problems. Your life is your own."

Now Samantha was beginning to get angry. "You don't care what happens to me," she said angrily, "as long as you keep on having a good time. And what's all this you keep saying about 'your women'? How many women are you seeing anyway?"

For the first time John Paul began to look uncomfortable and a little nervous. He tried to put back his usual smile and took her hand. "What difference does it make how many women I see? You're here with me now, aren't you? We have fun together and we can keep on having fun."

Samantha stared at him.

"It would be a lot easier without the baby," he continued, relaxing, "but if you did have the baby it wouldn't have much effect on me. I would still see you." He laughed. "See what a nice giy I am?"

"Oh, you're a real nice guy," said Samantha bitterly. "A real nice guy."

Chapter 15
A Difficult Choice

A Difficult Choice

Part 1

Vocabulary

These are the vocabulary words you will learn in this chapter. Each word has a definition and a sentence. Notice that many words have more than one meaning.

1. **blunt**
   1) (adjective)—not sharp
      A small child should use a blunt scissors.
   2) (adjective)—simple, direct, said without worrying about the other person's feelings; **bluntly** (adverb)—in a very direct, simple way
      *I want to know what you really think of the story; please
         be blunt.*
      If you are too blunt with Nga you may hurt her feelings.
      "Grandpa is dead," he said bluntly.

2. **regret** (verb)—to feel sorry about; (noun)—a feeling of being sorry
   *In 1776 Nathan Hale said, "I only regret that I have but one life to
      lose for my country."*
   I hope you feel regret for the miserable way you acted.

3. **distract** (verb)—to take attention away from what you're doing;
   distracted (adjective)
   If Tom turns the TV on, it will distract his son from his homework.
   *She was so distracted by thinking about her sick infant, that she
      couldn't concentrate on her work.*

4. **mess**
   1) (noun)—a lot of things mixed up, out of place, sometimes dirty;
      (verb)—to make things out of order
      We're not going out until you clean up the mess you made in the
        kitchen.
      The party really messed up the house; there are cups and little
        plates of food everywhere!
   2) (noun)—trouble, confusion
      The school was really in a mess when four teachers suddenly
        left in the same week.
      He got himself into a mess when he stole a car.

5. **total**
   1) (noun)—everything added together; (verb)—to add everything
      together
      The price is the total of everything you bought.
      The bill totals $9.75
   2) (adjective)—complete, whole; **totally** (adverb)—completely
      I'm going to clean all day; this house is a total mess.
      I was totally surprised when they told me I was to replace Alan
        as director.

6. **uninterested** (adjective)—not interested
   The teacher says that Mary is restless in class and seems
     uninterested in her school work.

7. **immediately** (adverb)—quickly, without waiting
   Call your son's school immediately.

8. **business** (noun)
   1) work, occupation; place for work or selling; selling
      Selling clothes is my business.
      She owns her own business on Main Street.
      Rainy days are not good for business; everyone stays home.
   2) personal concerns or interests [see Idioms #3]
      What happens to my sister is my business too.
      This is no concern of yours; mind your own business.

9. **afford** (verb)
   1) to have enough money for
      I'll have to get a second job; otherwise I won't be able to afford the rent on my new apartment.
   2) to have enough time or strength for
      I get sick if I don't have enough sleep; I can't afford to stay up late.

10. **alive** (adjective)—living, not dead
    Both of my grandparents are still alive.

11. **offer** (verb)—to show you are willing to give or do something;
    (noun)—the thing or act a person is willing to give or do
    When her friends came to visit, she would offer them tea.
    He offered me $100 for my piano.
    She was happy about his offer to help her move.
    Jill accepted Steve's offer of marriage.

12. **depend** (verb)
    1) to trust; to trust to give support or help
       You can depend on Sally to be here on time.
       Mrs. Harrison depends on her grandson to drive her to the supermarket every week.
    2) **depends on**—to be decided by
       Whether I can go to the movies or not depends on how much money I have.

Idioms

Idioms are words that have special meanings in English when used together.

1. **get rid of**—to make go away or throw away
   I've tried everything, but I can't get rid of this cold.
   If the piano won't fit into the new house, we may have to get rid of it.

2. **each other** — one person or thing to another person or thing

   Allan and Robin like to talk to each other.

   The two cars hit each other in the rain.

3. **none of his (my, your, her) business** — not his (my, your, her) concern

   [see Vocabulary #8]

   It's none of his business what I do with my money.

   What the guy in the next apartment does is none of my business.

4. **that much** — so much, very much

   That new law will not affect us that much.

Part 2

Vocabulary

Complete each of the following sentences with one of the words on the list. Don't forget to read the words before the blank *and* the words after the blank to help you find the missing vocabulary word.

Remember that all the answers (a, b, c) under one number are different meanings of the same word. When a word has more than one meaning, there is a parenthesis ( ) after the sentence. In the parenthesis put the number of the meaning from the vocabulary list in Part 1.

depend	regret
blunt	offer
alive	total
mess	afford
uninterested	distract
immediately	business

1. The noise from the street _____ (ed) the class, and they

   stopped paying attention to the teacher.

2. a) She added all the numbers to get the _____ . ( )

   b) When the lights went out, we were left in _____ dark-

   ness. ( )

3. a) I tried to tell her about her mistake in a gentle way, but when

   she didn't understand I had to be _____ . ( )

   b) She had trouble cutting the meat because the knife was so

   _____ . ( )

4. a) After she lost her job and her husband left her, her life was a

   _____ . ( )

   b) He was in such a rush to leave this morning that he left a

   _____ in the bedroom. ( )

5. He was badly hurt in the accident, but at least he's still _____ .

6. I can _____ you $1,000 for your car.

7. a) He has two _____ (es), a laundromat and a shoe store. ( )

   b) Don't get entangled in Janet's fight with her brother; it's not

   your _____ . ( )

8. He was _____ in the movie, so he left.

9. a) An infant has to _____ on its mother or father for

   everything. ( )

   b) Whether I go to the party _____ (s) on whether I get a

   babysitter. ( )

10. It was an emergency, so he left _____ .

11. a) He can't _____ to buy a new car. ( )

    b) I would like to go to the meeting, but I can't _____ the

    time. ( )

12. I _____ buying this car. It's always giving me trouble.

Idioms

Complete each of the following sentences with one of the idioms on the
list. Don't forget to read the words before the blank *and* the words
after the blank to help you with the missing idioms.

that much
each other
get rid of
none of his business

1. The two children like to play with _____ .

2. This place is a mess; we have to _____ some

   of these papers.

3. Hurry, we don't have _____ time before we

   leave.

4. When he asked me personal questions about my marriage, I became

   uncomfortable and told him it was _____ .

Part 3

Summary

Bradley has left Samantha for Gloria. Samantha is going out with John
Paul when she finds out she is pregnant by her husband Bradley. She
asks John Paul to help her decide what to do but he doesn't want to
get involved in her problems.

Questions to think and talk about before you read:

- Now that Samantha can't expect any help from John Paul,
  what do you think she will do?
- How do you think David will react when he hears about
  Samantha's pregnancy?

Episode 15. A Difficult Choice

"What's the matter with you, Samantha?" asked David as
Jasmine, David, and Samantha sat eating lunch in the hospital. "You're
so distracted. What's bothering you?"

Samantha and Jasmine looked at each other. "Go on, Jasmine," said Samantha in a tired voice. "You tell him."

Jasmine hesitated and then she said bluntly, "Samantha's pregnant, and Bradley's the father."

David stared at Samantha in shock. "Oh, Samantha," he said finally, "how can I help?"

Samantha smiled weakly. "It's enough for now that you're offering to help. All John Paul could say about it was that it was none of his business. He was totally uninterested in how I was feeling. I talked to him last week."

"Have you decided what you're going to do?" asked Jasmine.

"Well, John Paul is no help. I can't depend on him for anything." She sighed and put her head in her hands. "The only thing to do is just have an abortion. It's the simplest thing, the easiest, and then it would be all over."

"Oh, no," said David, putting his hand on her arm, "don't do that, Samantha. It's a baby; you can't get rid of it."

"It's not a baby yet," answered Samantha. "It's not really even alive yet."

"Just because it's small doesn't mean it isn't alive," answered David earnestly. "I think you'd regret it later if you had an abortion."

"But how could I afford a baby?" asked Samantha. "I don't make that much money. I'm all alone. Who would take care of it when I went to work? And I don't know anything about taking care of babies. What kind of life could I give a child when my own life is a mess?"

"I'm not trying to push you into anything," answered David. "I just want you to know that I'll help you however I can."

Samantha smiled at him. "Thanks," she said. "You and Jasmine are really good friends."

"Excuse me," said a voice next to Samantha. She looked up to see one of the secretaries in her office. "Samantha, you have a message from Bradley. He said to call him immediately."

Part 4

Questions

1. What did David notice about Samantha?
2. Who tells him about the problem?
3. What does David say when he hears the news?
4. How is what David says different from what John Paul said when he was told about Samantha's pregnancy?
5. What does Samantha think she wants to do? Why?
6. What does David say about what Samantha wants to do?
7. What are two of David's reasons?
8. What are two of Samantha's reasons?
9. What do you think Samantha should do?
10. At the end of the story, who has called Samantha? Why do you think he called her?

Part 5

Fill in the blanks with words from the vocabulary list. On the left are the letters of the word you need, but the letters are not in the correct order.

1. mdmieatiyle — quickly   _____

2. aottl — complete   _____

3. rtidsctade — not paying attention   _____

4. ulbtn — saying what you think in a direct way   _____

5. ialve — living   _____

6. efofr — to say you'll do something   _____

7. ssem — things mixed up and confused   _____

8. sesubins — place of work   _____

9. detseretninu — not concerned   _____

10. pedned — If you need someone you   _____

    _____ on him.

11. egrert — to feel sorry   _____

12. rfafod — to have enough money   _____

Part 6

There are eight vocabulary words spelled incorrectly in this copy of the story. Find the mistakes and correct them. The first one has been done for you.

"What's the matter with you, Samantha?" asked David as

Jasmine, David, and Samantha sat eating lunch in the hospital. "You're

so ~~ditracted~~. What's bothering you?"
    distracted

Samantha and Jasmine looked at each other. "Go on, Jasmine,"

said Samantha in a tired voice. "You tell him."

Jasmine hesitated and then she said blontly, "Samantha's preg-

nant, and Bradley's the father."

David stared at Samantha in shock. "Oh, Samantha," he said fi-

nally, "how can I help?"

Samantha smiled weakly. "It's enough for now that you're ofering

to help. All John Paul could say about it was that it was none of his

bussiness. He was totally uninterested in how I was feeling. I talked to

him last week."

"Have you decided what you're going to do?" asked Jasmine.

"Well, John Paul is no help. I can't depind on him for anything."

She sighed and put her head in her hands. "The only thing to do is just

have an abortion. It's the simplest thing, the easiest, and then it would

be all over."

"Oh, no," said David, putting his hand on her arm, "don't do that, Samantha. It's a baby; you can't get rid of it."

"It's not a baby yet," answered Samantha. "It's not really even alive yet."

"Just because it's small doesn't mean it isn't alive," answered David earnestly. "I think you'd regrit it later if you had an abortion."

"But how could I afor a baby?" asked Samantha. "I don't make that much money. I'm all alone. Who would take care of it when I went to work? And I don't know anything about taking care of babies. What kind of life could I give a child when my own life is a mess?"

"I'm not trying to push you into anything," answered David. "I just want you to know that I'll help you however I can."

Samantha smiled at him. "Thanks," she said. "You and Jasmine are really good friends."

"Excuse me," said a voice next to Samantha. She looked up to see one of the secretaries in her office. "Samantha, you have a message from Bradley. He said to call him imediately."

Review for Chapters **11–15**

Making Decisions

Part 1

Making Decisions

Questions to think and talk about before you read:

- How do you make an important decision?

The characters in this story have had a lot of decisions to make. Bradley had to decide whether or not to leave Samantha. Samantha had to decide whether to continue to see John Paul. Now she has to decide what to do about her pregnancy. All of us have to make decisions like these every day. How do we make them? Are there things that can help us decide?

Some people like to be alone when they are trying to make a decision. Other people find it helpful to talk over the problem with a friend or family member, as Samantha did when she talked to Jasmine and David. Talking to another person can sometimes help your own ideas, or *opinions*, become *clearer*, or easier to see or understand. A friend can sometimes help you see your problem from a different *point of view*, or way of looking at things. In the end, though, your sister or your husband or your friend cannot make the decision for you; Jasmine and David cannot make Samantha's decision for her. Although listening to everyone else's *opinions*, ideas, and feelings can help, in the end the final decision is yours to make.

Here are some steps that can be helpful when you're making a decision:

1. *List your choices, or options.* Making a list of your options can make your choices *clearer*, or easier to see. For example, if you want to buy a car and are deciding what kind to buy, you might have two choices on the list: a new car or a used car. Jasmine helped Samantha list her options: having and taking care of the baby by herself, going back to Bradley, having an abortion, giving the baby up for adoption, or marrying John Paul.

2. *List pros and cons.* Listing the *pros*, or good things, and *cons*, or bad things, about each option can be helpful and make the differences between your choices *clearer*. For example, when buying a used car a *pro* is that used cars are cheaper, a *con* is that used cars have more engine problems than a new car. A *pro* about Samantha going back to Bradley is that she would have help with the baby, a *con* is that Bradley acted badly toward her. Sometimes you will need to get more information to help you list your *pros* and *cons*. For example, you might go to the library to find out which are the best used cars. Samantha got some of the information she needed by talking to John Paul to find out if marrying him was a realistic option.

3. *Look at your feelings.* Look at the *pros*, or good things, and *cons*, or bad things, for each choice and see which of them is important to you and how you feel about each one. For example, if you find a used car that looks nice, is a reasonable price, and has a good engine, but it is very big and you hate to drive big cars, that is probably not the car for you. Even if Samantha can list many *pros* about giving up the baby for adoption, and her one *con* is that she will be miserable and bitter and regret it for the rest of her life, then she should not do it.

4. *Make the decision and accept it.* Once you have made your decision, agree to accept that option and do the best you can with it without feeling anxious about the choices you didn't take. For example, if you decide to buy a new car, you should try to accept that decision, and not waste a lot of time wondering if you should have paid that much money or if someone else has a better car. If Samantha decides to have and take care of the baby by herself, she should try to have the best life she can with that decision. She should try not to sit around wondering about the effect on her life if she had gone back to Bradley.

Part 2

Questions

1. Give one way talking to another person can help when you have a decision to make.

2. What is the first step in making a decision? How can it help?
3. What is the second step in making a decision? What is a pro for Samantha in going back to Bradley?
4. What is the third step in making a decision? Why is this good to do?
5. What is the fourth step in making a decision? Why do you think it's a bad idea to do a lot of thinking about the choices you didn't take?

Part 3

Vocabulary and Idioms

There are a few new words and idioms in what you have just read. You should be able to understand the meanings of these words by reading the words *before* and *after* them.

Fill in the blanks with the words that go with the definitions. If you're not sure of the meanings of the words, look back at the story. Usually the definition of the word is in the same sentence as the word.

con   point of view
pro   clearer
opinion

1. idea   _____

2. easier to see or understand   _____

3. good thing   _____

4. bad thing   _____

5. a way of looking at things   _____

Part 4

Vocabulary Review

This is a review of all the vocabulary words you have learned in Chapters 11-15. Match each word on the left with the definition on the right by putting the correct letter in the blank. Look back at the words in the chapters if you need help with any of the definitions.

Chapters 11–13

A.

1. stubborn _____	a. like
2. unusual _____	b. two
3. frightened _____	c. do
4. replace _____	d. seeing things the way they really are
5. interrupt _____	e. speak when someone else talks first
6. act _____	f. strange
7. realize _____	g. scared, afraid
8. couple _____	h. sad
9. examination _____	i. not willing to change
10. fact _____	j. thoughtful
11. miserable _____	k. choice, power to decide
12. realistic _____	l. to put one thing instead of another
13. option _____	m. understand what you didn't know before
14. enjoy _____	n. something true
15. pensive _____	o. looking at something carefully

B.

1. defend _____	a. bad
2. preoccupied _____	b. bother
3. cafeteria _____	c. get better
4. consult _____	d. happening because of something else
5. infant _____	e. thinking of one thing and doing something else
6. annoy _____	f. connection between things

7. recognize   _____   g. baby

8. discuss   _____   h. not pay attention

9. relationship   _____   i. hurry

10. improve   _____   j. talk about

11. result   _____   k. to fight for, protect

12. adoption   _____   l. to look for information from

13. lousy   _____   m. know again

14. rush   _____   n. place to eat and serve yourself

15. ignore   _____   o. agreement to use as your own

Chapters 13-15

A.

1. uncomfortable   _____   a. to be sorry

2. immediately   _____   b. to take attention away

3. abortion   _____   c. upsetting surprise

4. affect   _____   d. place of work

5. disturb   _____   e. to cause a change

6. wipe   _____   f. to upset

7. afford   _____   g. rub clean

8. guy   _____   h. not relaxed in your mind

9. blunt   _____   i. quickly

10. offer   _____   j. operation to end a pregnancy

11. shock   _____   k. get mixed together and caught

12. distract   _____   l. have enough money for

13. business   _____   m. boy or man

14. entangle   _____   n. saying what you mean in a direct way

15. regret   _____   o. show you will give or help

B.

1. anxious	_____	a.	living
2. mess	_____	b.	in another way, differently
3. restless	_____	c.	showing you mean what you say
4. tissue	_____	d.	not interested
5. earnest	_____	e.	hold up, keep from falling
6. total	_____	f.	a lot of things mixed up, out of place
7. oversleep	_____	g.	not able to relax
8. uninterested	_____	h.	thin paper used to clean the nose
9. dawn	_____	i.	bad, sour taste
10. alive	_____	j.	to be slow to speak or act
11. support	_____	k.	trust to help
12. bitter	_____	l.	sleep late
13. depend	_____	m.	everything added together
14. otherwise	_____	n.	worried
15. hesitate	_____	o.	when the sun comes up

Part 5

Idioms

This is a review of all the idioms you have learned in Chapters 11-15. Match the part of the sentence on the left that goes together with the end of the sentence on the right by putting the correct letter in the blank.

Chapters 11-13

1. You said you agreed with me but now you say you agree with Rose. Whose . . . _____
2. It started raining at dawn and it's been raining ever . . . _____
3. We've walked far enough. Let's go . . . _____
4. When she needs you, you shouldn't run . . . _____
5. That loud noise is driving . . . _____
6. I forgot what I wanted to say. Never . . . _____
7. The doctor is going to give . . . _____
8. She plans to give the child . . . _____
9. You look upset. What's . . . _____
10. I'm tired of sitting. I need to get . . . _____
11. Oh . . . _____
12. Don't stop talking. Go . . . _____
13. I invited Rita and Elaine to come . . . _____

a. up and walk around.
b. no! I've locked my keys in the car.
c. on with what you were saying.
d. over to my house.
e. since.
f. the matter?
g. up for adoption.
h. side are you on?
i. me crazy.
j. out on her.
k. mind.
l. Morris a checkup.
m. back home now.

Chapters 14-15

1. What you do with your life is up . . . _____
2. I'm going to do what I think best no matter . . . _____

a. in at George's house.
b. long as it doesn't rain.

3. I'm going to get rid . . . _____

4. I go for a walk every day even . . . _____

5. Let's have chocolate. I don't like vanilla that . . . _____

6. I don't care if we study math or English first. What . . . _____

7. My problems are none of . . . _____

8. Of . . . _____

9. Let's not talk about that. It has nothing . . . _____

10. We'll have the picnic as . . . _____

11. The two girls talk to each . . . _____

12. I get in bed and fall . . . _____

13. On the way home let's stop . . . _____

c. other on the phone every night.
d. to you.
e. asleep listening to music.
f. his business.
g. to do with the decision we have to make right now.
h. of this old lamp and replace it with a new one.
i. difference does it make?
j. much.
k. course I'd like to have a good job.
l. what Bill says.
m. if it's cold.

Chapter 16

"What Am I Going to Tell Gloria?"

Chapter 16

"What Am I Going to Tell Gloria?"

Part 1

Vocabulary

These are the vocabulary words you will learn in this chapter. Each word has a definition and a sentence. Notice that many words have more than one meaning.

1. **firm**
   1) (adjective)—strong, not easily moved
      The tree stands firm in the ground.
   2) (adjective)—sure, will not change her ideas; **firmly** (adverb)
      The teacher is firm about the children following the rules.
      *"If you make a mess with these tissues, you will stay after
         school," said the teacher firmly.*
   3) (adjective)—not soft when touched
      Because she exercises, her muscles are firm.
   4) (noun)—a group of people in business together
      That firm makes computers.

2. **silence** (noun)—complete quiet; (verb)—to make someone or something quiet
   They looked at each other in silence.
   He silenced the radio by turning it off.

3. **hysterical** (adjective)
   1) funny
      The hysterical movie made Sarah laugh until her stomach hurt.
   2) so upset that a person cannot hold back his feelings, and often cannot stop laughing or crying
      The child became hysterical at her mother's funeral and they had to take her home.

4. **order**
   1) (verb)—to tell a person what he must do; (noun)—something telling a person what he must do, a command
      The policeman ordered the car to stop.
      You must obey when the general gives you an order.
   2) (verb)—to ask for something in a store or restaurant; (noun)—a request for something in a store or restaurant
      I ordered a new sofa but it won't be ready until next week.
      You can give an order to the store by phone.
   3) (noun)—a paper saying money is to be paid
      I sent him a money order.
   4) (noun)—things in their correct place
      Put these numbers in order from smallest to largest.
      After the party it took us all day to put the house back in order.
   5) **out of order** (idiom)—broken
      The washing machine was out of order so we couldn't use it.

5. **groan** (noun)—a low sound a person makes when in pain or when sad or disappointed; (verb)—to make such a sound
   When the doctor touched her broken arm, she gave a groan.
   "Oh no!" groaned Larry when he heard the bad news.

6. **separate** (verb)—to divide; to go in different places or directions
   Separate the books into two piles.
   The woman and her husband are going to separate.

7. **irritate** (verb)
   1) to bother or annoy
      Loud noises early in the morning irritate me.
   2) to bother a part of the body; to make it hurt
      This sweater irritates my skin.

8. **impulsive** (adjective)—sudden acting from your feelings without thinking; (adverb)—suddenly acting from your feelings
The impulsive boy gave all his money to the homeless man.
"Let's all get up at dawn and go to the beach!" she said impulsively.

9. **roll**
   1) (verb)—to turn over and over; to move along by turning over
   Horses like to roll over in the dirt.
   The children roll the ball along.
   When she started to cry, a tear rolled down her face.
   2) (verb)—to make something long and round by turning over and over; (noun)—something turned over in a round shape
   Roll up the paper.
   Please give me a roll of toilet paper.
   3) (verb)—to make flat by turning something over and over on it
   The woman rolled the flour and water flat with a bottle before she cut the cookies.
   4) (noun)—a small, individual bread
   He bought a dozen rolls at the bakery.

10. **perfect** (adjective)—very good, cannot be made better
It's a perfect day for the beach.
His typing was perfect.

11. **breathe** (verb)
    1) to take air in and let it out
    The doctor told her to breathe in and out.
    2) whisper
    Her boyfriend breathed words of love.

12. **breath**
    1. (noun)—the air you take in and let out
    The day was so cold that the girl could see her breath.
    2) **under your breath** (idiom)—in a whisper
    He talked to his friend under his breath so the teacher couldn't hear.

3) **to hold your breath** (idiom) — to stop breathing, often from excitement or fear
   Hold your breath when you jump in the water.
   The policeman held his breath when the robber pulled out a gun.

Idioms

Idioms are words that have special meanings in English when used together.

1. **to get back together** — to come together again as they were before
   I'm happy to see Mary and her sister get back together again after their fight.

2. **mouth fell open** — when a person opens his mouth without planning to out of surprise or shock
   Her mouth fell open when she saw an elephant on Main Street.

3. **the thing is** — the idea is, what I really mean is . . .
   You never clean up. The thing is, I'm the one who has to do all the cleaning.

4. **get to the point** — say what you really mean; used when a person is not direct about what he wants to say
   This story is too long. Get to the point.

5. **oh, brother** — an expression of regret you say when something upsetting has happened
   Oh, brother, Mother will be furious when she finds out what I've done.

Part 2

Vocabulary

Complete each of the following sentences with one of the vocabulary words on the list. Don't forget to read the words before the blank *and* the words after the blank to help you find the missing vocabulary word.

Remember that all the answers (a, b, c) under one number are different meanings of the same word. When a word has more than one meaning, there is a parenthesis ( ) after the sentence. In the parenthesis put the number of the meaning from the vocabulary list in Part 1.

hysterical	order
firm	silence
roll	groan
irritate	separate
breathe	impulsive
breath	perfect

1. a) Please put these words in alphabetical _____. ( )

   b) Let's call up and _____ a pizza. ( )

   c) In the army a soldier must follow _____(s). ( )

   d) This telephone is out of _____. ( )

   e) I went to the post office to get a money _____ for $10.00. ( )

2. We are going to _____ the girls and boys into different groups.

3. a) Tomatoes should be _____, not soft. ( )

   b) When she disciplines her daughter, she speaks in a _____ voice. ( )

   c) Make sure the ladder is standing _____ before you climb it. ( )

   d) The bank she works for is a big _____. ( )

4. a) The pen _____(ed) down the desk and fell to the floor. ( )

   b) The children _____(ed) the clay into flat pancakes. ( )

   c) I like a _____ and butter with dinner. ( )

   d) Please _____ up the blanket. ( )

5. a) Cigarette smoke _____(s) my eyes. ( )

   b) I was _____(d) that she was so late. ( )

6. a) When the woman saw her child get hit by a car she became

      _____ and they couldn't calm her down. ( )

   b) George couldn't stop laughing at the _____ joke. ( )

7. Her test paper was _____ ; she got all the answers

   right.

8. The pain was so bad that he gave a loud _____ .

9. I need complete _____ when I'm studying.

10. Even though it was very cold out, the _____ girl suddenly

    stopped and gave her coat to a friend.

11. a) The smell in the room was so bad that he had to hold his

       _____ . ( )

    b) She took a deep _____ before jumping into the water. ( )

    c) I couldn't hear what he said because he said it under his

       _____ . ( )

12. a) He went to Vermont on his vacation because he liked to

       _____ the clean mountain air. ( )

    b) She _____(d) the words into his ear. ( )

Idioms

Complete each of the following sentences with one of the idioms on the
list. Don't forget to read the words before the blank *and* the words after
the blank to help you find the missing idiom.

mouth fell open	get back together
the thing is	get to the point
oh, brother	

1. His _____ when they told him he had won a

   million dollars.

2. You've been talking for a long time and I still don't understand what

   you want me to do. Please _____ .

3. The little boy wished that his divorced parents would

   _____ again.

4. She's late. _____ , if she doesn't come soon,

   we'll have to leave.

5. _____ , I overslept and now I'm late to work.

Part 3

Summary

Bradley has left Samantha for Gloria. Samantha is going out with John Paul when she discovers she is pregnant by her husband Bradley. John Paul wants to stay out of it, Samantha talks things over with her friends Jasmine and David, and Bradley asks her to call him.

Questions to think about and discuss before you read:

- How do you think Bradley and Samantha will feel when they see each other now?
- Have you or someone you know ever laughed and cried at the same time?

Episode 16. "What Am I Going to Tell Gloria?"

Samantha called Bradley as soon as she got back from lunch. "I don't want to discuss this on the phone," he said. "Can I come over later and talk to you?"

"I'll meet you in the hospital cafeteria," replied Samantha impulsively, "not at home."

After ordering coffee and sitting down in the cafeteria, Bradley and Samantha looked at each other nervously.

"Well," said Samantha, "what is it?"

Bradley sat back in his chair and looked at his hands. "You and I have been separated for over a month now. I don't think we'll ever get back together again, do you?"

"No," she said firmly.

"The thing is," continued Bradley nervously, "I love Gloria." He looked at her.

"Oh really, Bradley," said Samantha in an irritated voice, "you told me that in the second episode. What is it? Get to the point."

He took a deep breath. "I'll be blunt with you, Samantha," he said. "I want a divorce. I want to marry Gloria."

There was silence for a moment. A tear rolled down Samantha's face and then, suddenly, she started to laugh. "Oh that's perfect," she gasped, laughing so hard she could hardly breathe. "That's just perfect."

"What's the matter with you?" asked Bradley as Samantha continued to laugh loudly and people started to stare at them. "You're hysterical."

"I'm not just hysterical," she answered, laughing and crying at the same time. "I'm pregnant, eight weeks pregnant."

"Pregnant!" said Bradley angrily. "You didn't waste much time, did you?"

"You didn't hear me," said Samantha, suddenly serious. "I said *eight weeks* pregnant."

Bradley thought for a minute, and then his mouth fell open. "You mean . . . you mean it's my baby?"

"Our baby," answered Samantha, starting to cry now for real.

"Oh, brother," groaned Bradley, "what am I going to tell Gloria?"

Part 4

Questions

1. Where does Samantha meet Bradley?
2. Why does Bradley look at his hands?
3. Why doesn't Bradley tell Samantha what he wants right away?
4. What does he want?

5. What is Samantha's first reaction when he tells her? What is her second reaction?
6. What does she mean when she says, "That's perfect"?
7. Why does she get a little hysterical?
8. What does Bradley mean by, "You didn't waste much time, did you?" Do you think that he has a right to be angry?
9. What does Bradley say when he finds out he's the father of the baby?
10. What do you think Bradley will do now?

Part 5

Complete this crossword with words from your vocabulary list.

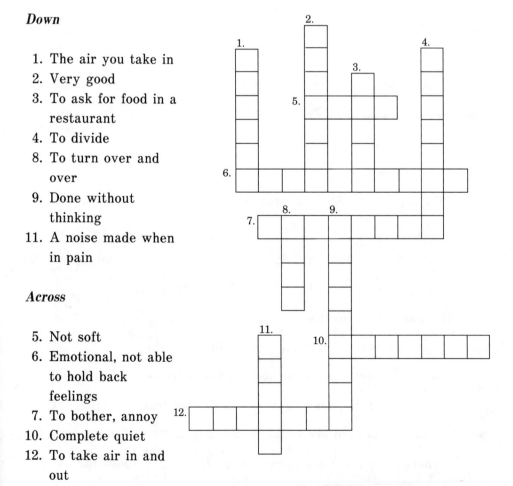

Down

1. The air you take in
2. Very good
3. To ask for food in a restaurant
4. To divide
8. To turn over and over
9. Done without thinking
11. A noise made when in pain

Across

5. Not soft
6. Emotional, not able to hold back feelings
7. To bother, annoy
10. Complete quiet
12. To take air in and out

Part 6

There are nine vocabulary words spelled incorrectly in this copy of the story. Find the mistakes and correct them. The first one has been done for you.

Samantha called Bradley as soon as she got back from lunch. "I don't want to discuss this on the phone," he said. "Can I come over later and talk to you?"

"I'll meet you in the hospital cafeteria," replied Samantha
impulsively
~~impulsivly~~, "not at home."

After ordering coffee and sitting down in the cafeteria, Bradley and Samantha looked at each other nervously.

"Well," said Samantha, "what is it?"

Bradley sat back in his chair and looked at his hands. "You and I have been seperated for over a month now. I don't think we'll ever get back together again, do you?"

"No," she said firmly.

"The thing is," continued Bradley nervously, "I love Gloria." He looked at her.

"Oh really, Bradley," said Samantha in an irittated voice, "you told me that in the second episode. What is it? Get to the point."

He took a deep breathe. "I'll be blunt with you, Samantha," he said. "I want a divorce. I want to marry Gloria."

There was silence for a moment. A tear roled down Samantha's face and then, suddenly, she started to laugh. "Oh that's perfect," she gasped, laughing so hard she could hardly breath. "That's just perfict."

"What's the matter with you?" asked Bradley as Samantha continued to laugh loudly and people started to stare at them. "You're histeracal."

"I'm not just hysterical," she answered, laughing and crying at the same time. "I'm pregnant, eight weeks pregnant."

"Pregnant!" said Bradley angrily. "You didn't waste much time, did you?"

"You didn't hear me," said Samantha, suddenly serious. "I said *eight weeks* pregnant."

Bradley thought for a minute, and then his mouth fell open. "You mean . . . you mean it's my baby?"

"Our baby," answered Samantha, starting to cry now for real.

"Oh, brother," groned Bradley, "what am I going to tell Gloria?"

Chapter 17
Bradley's Solution

Bradley's Solution

Part 1

Vocabulary

These are the vocabulary words you will learn in this chapter. Each word has a definition and a sentence. Notice that many words have more than one meaning.

1. **soothing** (adjective)—bringing relief, comfort, calm
   The soothing cream made his sunburn feel better.
   When the man groaned in pain, the nurse spoke to him in a soothing voice.

2. **eager** (adjective)—wanting very much
   I was eager to get my sister's opinion of my new dress, so I called her immediately.

3. **scream** (noun)—a high, long, loud cry or yell; (verb)—to make a high, long, loud cry
   Suddenly we were distracted by a loud scream coming from the butcher shop.
   After he fell we heard him scream in pain.

4. **sink** (past tense—sank)
   1) (verb)—to go down, usually slowly
      As the balloon lost air, it started to sink.
      When she heard the bad news, she sank slowly into a chair.

2) (verb)—to go down in water, or cause to go down in water

*Because she couldn't swim, she started to sink and we had to
jump in and save her.*

*During the war, their navy tried to sink the boats in
our navy.*

3) (verb)—to go deeply

Wipe up the milk that fell before it sinks into the rug.

*It took a few minutes for the bad news to sink in, and then she
started to cry.*

4) (noun)—a large container used for washing

Augustin went to the sink to wash his hands.

5. **impatient** (adjective)—not patient, not willing to wait, restless

*She was so impatient to be out of the supermarket, that she impul-
sively took the food from the clerk and put it in the bag herself.*

6. **solution** (noun)

1) an answer to a problem

It took me an hour to find the solution to this math problem.

2) liquid chemical mixture

*Take this solution after eating so it doesn't irritate your
stomach.*

7. **fold**

1) (verb)—to bend part of something over the other part;
(noun)—the part that has been bent over

I fold the laundry before I put it away in the dresser.

Make three folds in your paper.

2) (verb)—bend close to the body

Mary Ellen folded her arms and stood in angry silence.

Brenda sat with her legs folded under her.

3) (verb)—to mix gently

Fold the raisins into the mixture.

8. **abandon** (verb)—to leave or give up completely

When the ship started to sink, the captain decided to abandon ship.

*When Molly's idea didn't work, she abandoned it and tried some-
thing different.*

9. **raise**
   1) (verb)—pick up, make higher; (noun)—higher pay or price
      He raised the flag above his head.
      The landlord is going to raise the rent.
      With my raise in pay, I can afford to buy a car.
   2) (verb)—bring together, collect
      The church is trying to raise money.
      In times of war, the government will raise a larger army.
   3) (verb)—help to grow, bring up
      *After his wife died, Henry depended on his sister to help him
         raise his two daughters.*
      I'm going to raise tomatoes in my garden this year.

10. **reach**
    1) (verb)—to be able to touch, to try and touch; (noun)—the distance
       it takes to touch
       Irena tried to reach one of the apples on the tree.
       *I know when my children want to be picked up, because they
          reach out their arms to me.*
       Joanne put a glass of water in reach of her bed.
    2) (verb)—to arrive at, get to
       We reached Chicago at 8:00 P.M.
       Drinking alcohol is legal when you reach the age of 21.
       After calling Peter several times, I finally reached him.

11. **handle**
    1) (noun)—the part of something you hold with your hand
       Knives, suitcases, spoons, and cups all have handles.
    2) (verb)—to touch or hold with your hand
       Please don't handle the tomatoes.
       Please handle with care.
    3) (verb)—use, manage, control
       I offered to teach him how to handle a truck.
       She doesn't know how to handle her children.
       These problems are too much for me to handle.

12. **resist** (verb)—to hold back against, fight against
    She resisted when he tried to pull her out the door.
    The fat woman tried to resist eating the chocolate cake.

Idioms

Idioms are words that have special meanings in Engish when used together.

1. **make it up** — to think up a story that is not true, to lie
   I don't believe the excuse he gave. I think he made it up.

2. **turn her back** — when someone turns so her back is to you, showing she is angry and doesn't want to speak
   "Nobody's perfect! Please don't be angry," I said earnestly, but he just turned his back on me.

3. **all right** — for certain, used to make what you just said stronger
   I'm hungry all right; I could eat a horse!

4. **what about me? (him, her, that)** — have you thought about me (him, her, that)?
   You called everyone else and invited them to the party. What about me?
   You seem completely uninterested in what happens to Laura. What about her?
   You said everything was fixed, but the sink is still broken. What about that?

5. **the hell with you** — you can go to hell, showing you're angry at someone and are dismissing him
   I don't care what you do anymore — the hell with you.
   I'm tired of trying to fix this sink. The hell with it; I'm calling the plumber.

Part 2

Vocabulary

Complete each of the following sentences with one of the words on the list. Don't forget to read the words before the blank *and* the words after the blank to help you find the missing vocabulary word.

Remember that all the answers (a, b, c) under one number are different meanings of the same word. When a word has more than one meaning, there is a parenthesis ( ) after the sentence. In the parenthesis put the number of the meaning from the vocabulary list in Part 1.

soothing	sink
abandon	solution
reach	eager
raise	resist
handle	fold
scream	impatient

1. a) When I couldn't _____ him by phone, I wrote him a

    letter. ( )

   b) I tried to get my scarf down from the top of the closet, but I

    couldn't _____ it. ( )

2. a) Please put your dishes in the _____ . ( )

   b) On a hot day the rain _____ (s) quickly into the dry

    earth. ( )

   c) If you put a brick in a pail of water, it will _____ to the

    bottom. ( )

   d) At sunset, the sun _____ (s) slowly down behind the

    mountains. ( )

3. a) Don't worry, I have a _____ to the problem. ( )

   b) He washed his mouth with a _____ of salt and water. ( )

4. When I'm in a hurry to get home and the traffic is bad, I get

    _____ .

5. a) When a child answers a question in school, he must _____

    his hand. ( )

   b) We all try to _____ our children in the best way that

    we can. ( )

c) In order to build the new hospital, we must _____ money. ( )

6. When the enemy attacked, the people tried to _____ .

7. The calm, _____ music put him to sleep.

8. The desperate woman decided to _____ her child on the doorstep of the church.

9. He's always _____ to get home from work on Friday.

10. a) When she's impatient, she _____ (s) her arms across her chest. ( )

    b) You need to _____ the paper before putting it in the envelope. ( )

    c) After adding the milk, _____ the eggs into the cake batter. ( )

11. a) The cup fell when its _____ broke. ( )

    b) Do you know how to _____ this kind of machine? ( )

    c) Kittens have to be _____ (d) carefully. ( )

12. She became hysterical and started to _____ when she saw her son get hit by a car.

Idioms

Complete each of the following sentences with one of the idioms on the list. Don't forget to read the words before the blank *and* the words after the blank to help you find the missing idioms.

turned her back	made it up
what about me?	all right
the hell with you	

1. "I don't want to talk about it anymore," she said as she _____

   _____ .

2. He doesn't really have a rich father. He _____ .

3. I never want to see you again. _____ .

4. You ate all the food, and now I come home and there's nothing left.

   _____ .

5. I'm tired _____ , and I'm going straight to

   bed.

Part 3

Summary

Bradley has left Samantha for Gloria. Samantha is going out with John Paul when she discovers she is pregnant by her husband Bradley. John Paul wants to keep out of it, and Samantha tells Bradley she is pregnant.

Questions to think and talk about before you read:

- What do you think Gloria will say when Bradley tells her Samantha is pregnant?
- What do you think Bradley's solution to the problem will be?

Episode 17. Bradley's Solution

Bradley drove slowly to Gloria's house. He had told Samantha that he needed to think, and that's just what he was doing. By the time he reached Gloria's house, he knew what he was going to do.

"Did you tell her?" asked Gloria as she opened the door for him.

"I told her," answered Bradley, walking into the living room, "but she had something to tell me, too." He turned to Gloria, took a breath, and looked firmly into her eyes. "Samantha's pregnant, and I'm the father of the baby."

"What!" cried Gloria, sinking into a chair. "I don't believe it! She made it up just to get you to go back to her."

"It's true all right," replied Bradley. "But don't worry. I've thought of a solution to the whole problem." He smiled eagerly and sat down next to her. "I'll still divorce Samantha and marry you. Then as soon as the baby is born, you and I will take it and raise it. I'll have my son, you can adopt him, and everybody will be happy."

"Everybody will be happy?" exclaimed Gloria. "You'll be happy, but what about me? What makes you think I want to raise another woman's child? And how do you know Samantha would give the child up? Did you ask her?"

Bradley took her hands and tried to hug her, but she resisted. "Don't worry, I can handle Samantha. Don't you want a baby that's a part of me?" he said in a soothing voice.

"I want a baby that's a part of you, but I want it to be my baby, not hers—mine!" yelled Gloria. "And how do you know it will be a son, anyway?"

"Please, Gloria," said Bradley, beginning to get impatient, "this is the best solution for everyone."

"It's only the best solution for you. I will never agree to it!" She sat back and folded her arms.

Now Bradley was angry. "It's my child and I'm not going to abandon it!" he cried, jumping to his feet. "If you won't agree to take the baby, then I'll go back to Samantha and have my son with her!"

"What son?!" screamed Gloria.

"My son!" cried Bradley as he walked angrily toward the door. "Mine and Samantha's!"

"Then go to her," yelled Gloria as she turned her back, "and the hell with you!"

Part 4

Questions

1. What does Bradley tell Gloria?
2. What does Gloria say to Bradley's news?

3. What is Bradley's solution to the problem?
4. Does Gloria think this is a good solution? Why or why not?
5. Do you think Samantha would agree to Bradley's solution? Why or why not?
6. How is Gloria feeling?
7. Why do you think Bradley believes the baby will be a boy?
8. At the end of the story, how is Bradley feeling?
9. What does Bradley decide to do at the end of the story?

Part 5

Look back at the word list to help you find and circle the twelve vocabulary words in the puzzle. The words can be spelled forward or backward, and in any direction. There are also two extra words from the story, *exclaim* and *reply*. See if you can find all fourteen words. One word has been done for you.

```
S I J L T B D A R S P E F R S Y
H A N D L E R H I O M A D E B R
F A C A A R S C C L E G P N M L
S H R N M O F A H U F E L B E R
T I M P A T I E N T G R E P L Y
E S N M B T R R C I D E A A C H
Z C R K A F G E S O O T H I N G
E R B G N H L S A N L S R A S A
N E O S D D F I B M I A L C X E
M A N F O L D S Q P N G F D E C
B M J H N R I T S B A D O P T L
```

Part 6

There are nine vocabulary words spelled incorrectly in this copy of the story. Find the mistakes and correct them. The first one has been done for you. One word has been spelled wrong twice.

Bradley drove slowly to Gloria's house. He had told Samantha
that he needed to think, and that's just what he was doing. By the time
he ~~reeehed~~ Gloria's house, he knew what he was going to do.
_{reached}

"Did you tell her?" asked Gloria as she opened the door for him.

"I told her," answered Bradley, walking into the living room, "but
she had something to tell me, too." He turned to Gloria, took a breath,
and looked firmly into her eyes. "Samantha's pregnant, and I'm the father of the baby."

"What!" cried Gloria, sincking into a chair. "I don't believe it! She
made it up just to get you to go back to her."

"It's true all right," replied Bradley. "But don't worry. I've
thought of a solucion to the whole problem." He smiled egerly and sat
down next to her. "I'll still divorce Samantha and marry you. Then as
soon as the baby is born, you and I will take it and raese it. I'll have
my son, you can adopt him, and everybody will be happy."

"Everybody will be happy?" exclaimed Gloria. "You'll be happy,
but what about me? What makes you think I want to raise another
woman's child? And how do you know Samantha would give the child
up? Did you ask her?"

Bradley took her hands and tried to hug her, but she resissted.
"Don't worry, I can handle Samantha. Don't you want a baby that's a
part of me?" he said in a soothing voice.

"I want a baby that's a part of you, but I want it to be my baby,
not hers—mine!" yelled Gloria. "And how do you know it will be a son,
anyway?"

"Please, Gloria," said Bradley, beginning to get impacient, "this is
the best solution for everyone."

245 / Chapter 17

"It's only the best solushion for you. I will never agree to it!" She sat back and folded her arms.

Now Bradley was angry. "It's my child and I'm not going to abanden it!" he cried, jumping to his feet. "If you won't agree to take the baby, then I'll go back to Samantha and have my son with her!"

"What son?!" screamed Gloria.

"My son!" cried Bradley as he walked angrily toward the door. "Mine and Samantha's!"

"Then go to her," yelled Gloria as she turned her back, "and the hell with you!"

Chapter 18
Thinking for Herself

Chapter 18

Thinking for Herself

Part 1

Vocabulary

These are the vocabulary words you will learn in this chapter. Each word has a definition and a sentence. Notice that many words have more than one meaning.

1. **refuse** (verb)—to say no
   I refuse to answer you if you're going to scream at me.

2. **absolutely** (adverb)—completely
   I'm absolutely sure that this is the business for me.

3. **pleasant** (adjective)—nice, enjoyable
   We spent a pleasant day at my brother's house.

4. **announce** (verb)—tell in a formal way; make public
   Anibel and her boyfriend decided to announce their wedding plans to Anibel's mother.
   It was a total surprise when the police announced that the missing girl was alive.

5. **assume** (verb)—to believe something is true without being told it is so
   We always have rolls for dinner, so I assume we will have them tonight, too.
   I agreed with your point of view once or twice, but don't assume I always will.

6. **solemn** (adjective)—very serious, earnest; having importance, formal
   She looked solemn when she announced the important news.

7. **tense**
   1) (adjective)—nervous, tight; (verb)—to make tight; **tensely** (adverb)—nervously
      "Breathe deeply. It will make you feel less tense," said the coach to the nervous basketball players.
      We saw his muscles tense as the weight lifter raised 300 pounds.
      As she walked down the dark, lonely street, Nancy looked around tensely.
   2) (noun)—the form of the verb that shows when an action happened
      The past tense of "leave" is "left."

8. **suggest** (verb)—to offer an idea
   Louise suggested we separate the class into two groups.

9. **nut**
   1) (noun)—a small hard fruit that grows inside a hard shell; for example, peanuts, walnuts
      Lena likes to eat nuts and raisins.
   2) (noun)—a small piece of metal with a hole in it that keeps a screw in place
      There are two screws and two nuts that hold the handle of the door in place.
   3) (noun)—a person who does crazy things; **nuts** (adjective)—crazy
      Only a real nut would be so eager to play baseball in 100° weather.
      When we saw Sal singing and dancing on the table we thought he was nuts.
   4) (noun)—a person who likes someone or something very much; **nuts** (adjective)—liking someone or something very much
      Only a baseball nut would go to every single baseball game.
      Romeo was nuts about Juliet.

10. **demand**
    1) (verb)—to ask for strongly, to order as if you had a right to;
       (noun)—something asked for strongly; **demanding** (adjective)—
       asking for strongly, as if you had a right to
       *When she went through a red light, the policeman demanded
       that she stop and show him her driver's license.*
       The workers made a demand for more money.
       *He is a very demanding person; he wants you to do just what he
       says.*
       *Mary has a demanding job; she sometimes has to stay late just
       to keep up with the work.*
    2) **in demand**—asked for, wanted
       Good plumbers and electricians are always in demand.

11. **settle** (verb)
    1) to become comfortable
       The dog settled on the rug.
    2) to go to live in a place
       After traveling for many years, he settled in St. Louis, Missouri.
    3) to calm
       He thought a day in the country would help settle his nerves.
       Children, you're too wild. Settle down.
    4) to come to an agreement, decide
       *After talking it over to make their ideas clearer, Debbie and Pat
       settled on a better way to do the work.*

12. **collect**
    1) (verb)—to group or gather together
       *Bill collected his books, pencils, hat, and coat, and got ready to
       go home.*
       A crowd always collects when there is a fire.
       Sharon collects beautiful little boxes.
    2) (verb)—to take as payment
       I'm going to collect $2 from each of you to pay for the pizza.
    3) (verb)—to bring your feelings or thoughts together
       *He wrote down the pros and cons of leaving his job to help him
       collect his thoughts and come to a solution.*

4) (adjective); (adverb) — paid by the person receiving the phone call
or package
Will you accept a collect call from Mr. Ronald Coleman?
I called Mary Jane collect.

Idioms

Idioms are words that have special meanings in English when used
together.

1. **go off** — go away
Sylvia decided to go off by herself so she could think.

2. **at first** — in the beginning
*There is a famous saying, "If at first you don't succeed, try, try
again."*

3. **what's wrong with her?** — what's her problem? what's the matter
with her?
He never does his homework. What's wrong with him?

4. **around here** — here or near here
I haven't seen you around here before.

5. **just like that** — without thinking, without consideration
*I'm really angry at the way you left, just like that, without telling
anybody.*

Part 2

Vocabulary

Complete each of the following sentences with one of the words on the
list. Don't forget to read the words before the blank *and* the words after
the blank to help you find the missing vocabulary word.

Remember that all the answers (a, b, c) under one number are
different meanings of the same word. When a word has more than one

meaning, there is a parenthesis ( ) after the sentence. In the parenthesis put the number of the meaning from the vocabulary list in Part 1.

settle	tense
announce	pleasant
solemn	assume
demand	refuse
collect	absolutely
nut	suggest

1. A funeral is a _____ occasion.

2. a) The children decided to _____ the argument by asking
their mother. ( )

   b) He took some soothing medicine to _____ his
stomach. ( )

   c) When she came to the U.S., she decided to _____ in
Los Angeles. ( )

   d) When everyone had _____ (d) into their chairs, he
turned on the television. ( )

3. a) She likes to _____ stamps. ( )

   b) He calls his parents _____. ( )

   c) The bus driver held out his hand to _____ money from
the passengers. ( )

   d) She tried to _____ herself after the accident. ( )

4. I _____ that you use the dictionary if you don't understand
the meaning of a word.

5. a) Whenever I have to take a test, I get very _____ and
my muscles _____ up too. ( )

   b) In grammar we have the present and past _____ (s). ( )

6. When the senator decided to run for president, he _____(d) it to the newspapers.

7. Because the school was closed last year on Martin Luther King's birthday, I _____ it will be closed this year too.

8. Spring usually has _____ weather, not too cold or too hot.

9. a) The customer loudly _____(ed) her money back. ( )

   b) When Cabbage Patch dolls were first sold, they were in great _____. ( )

10. Are you _____ sure he's not coming?

11. He couldn't play football in school because his mother _____(d) to give permission.

12. a) She likes to break open the shell and eat the _____ inside. ( )

   b) Anyone who would go outside in the snow without a jacket, must be _____(s). ( )

   c) He's a real car _____; he spends all his time buying, fixing, and looking at cars. ( )

   d) A screw is often used with a _____. ( )

Idioms

Complete each of the following sentences with one of the idioms on the list. Don't forget to read the words before the blank *and* the words after the blank to help you find the missing idioms.

go off   at first
what's wrong with her?   around here
just like that

1. I can't find my watch, but I know it's _____ somewhere.

2. He decided to abandon his vacation plans and _____

   to visit his sister.

3. Mai is tense and angry. _____

4. He resisted our ideas _____, but finally he

   agreed with us.

5. She came in here without an appointment, _____

   _____, and demanded that the doctor see her immediately.

Part 3

Summary

Bradley has left Samantha for Gloria. Samantha is going out with John
Paul when she discovers she is pregnant by her husband Bradley.
Samantha tells Bradley and Bradley tells Gloria.

Questions to think and talk about before you read:

- Do you think Samantha will take Bradley back?
- In your opinion, *should* Samantha take Bradley back? Would you
  take him back if you were Samantha?

Episode 18. Thinking for Herself

Samantha had just gotten home from work when the doorbell
rang.

"Bradley!" she exclaimed when she opened the door. "What are
you doing here?"

"Samantha," said Bradley solemnly, as he walked into the house,
"I came to tell you some important news. I'm coming back to you."

"Oh, you are, are you?" replied Samantha after collecting her
thoughts for a moment. "And what makes you think I want you back?"

"I know it's been hard for you," said Bradley as he settled comfortably on the living room couch. "You must have been depressed thinking

about my being with Gloria, but now everything will be back the way it was." He looked around the living room. "I think we'll need some new curtains in here."

"Now wait a minute," said Samantha tensely. "You can't just come in here and assume that everything will be the same as before. You go off with Gloria, and then you announce that you're coming back, just like that! Depressed, ha! Who needs you!"

"But, Samantha," answered Bradley in a shocked voice, "didn't you miss me?"

"I did at first, because I was lonely," said Samantha thoughtfully, "but then I realized that it was a lot more pleasant around here without you. You're not easy to live with, you know. You're very demanding. And what about Gloria?"

"Demanding? Me?" asked a surprised Bradley. "I don't know what you mean. As for Gloria, she doesn't understand. When I suggested that she take the baby after you have it, she absolutely refused. I don't know what's wrong with her. So here I am."

Samantha stood completely still for a moment, and then she said wonderingly, "You're crazy, Bradley. You know, you really are nuts."

Bradley reached out a hand toward her. "But Samantha, what about the baby? Think of him. Doesn't he need both of us as parents? We should stay together for the baby."

"Yes, I've thought of that," answered Samantha quietly, sitting down. "Maybe for the good of the baby, I should take you back. I don't know. I have to think about it some more." She looked at him firmly. "You'll just have to wait until I decide what to do."

"What about what I think?" demanded Bradley. "I *am* the father."

"I spent our entire marriage listening to what you thought and doing only what you wanted. Now it's time for me to think for myself." She stood up and handed him his coat. "When I make my decision, I'll let you know."

Part 4

Questions

1. What does Bradley come to tell Samantha?
2. How does Bradley expect Samantha to react to his news?

3. Is Samantha happy to hear his news? How does she react?
4. How was life without Bradley for Samantha at first?
5. Why does Samantha say that, later, life was more pleasant without Bradley?
6. Samantha says Bradley is demanding. Does Bradley agree? Do you?
7. Why does Samantha say that Bradley is nuts?
8. When Samantha and Bradley were together, who usually made the decisions in their marriage?
9. Who's going to make the decision about Samantha's pregnancy? Do you think that's fair?
10. Samantha seems to have changed since she and Bradley were together. What do you think caused that to happen?

Part 5

Fill in the blanks with your vocabulary words.

1. A person who does something crazy is _____ (s).

2. What a person does who wants something *right now!* _____

3. If you won't do it, you _____ .

4. Completely and totally. _____

5. Nice. _____

6. To tell everyone the news. _____

7. Nervous or tight. _____

8. To sit down and get all comfortable. _____

9. To gather up a lot of things. _____

10. Serious, formal. _____

11. To believe to be true. _____

12. To give an idea. _____

Part 6

There are nine vocabulary words spelled incorrectly in this copy of the story. Find the mistakes and correct them. The first one has been done for you.

Samantha had just gotten home from work when the doorbell rang.

"Bradley!" she exclaimed when she opened the door. "What are you doing here?"

"Samantha," said Bradley ~~solemly~~ solemnly, as he walked into the house, "I came to tell you some important news. I'm coming back to you."

"Oh, you are, are you?" replied Samantha after colectting her thoughts for a moment. "And what makes you think I want you back?"

"I know it's been hard for you," said Bradley as he setled comfortably on the living room couch. "You must have been depressed thinking about my being with Gloria, but now everything will be back the way it was." He looked around the living room. "I think we'll need some new curtains in here."

"Now wait a minute," said Samantha tensely. "You can't just come in here and asume that everything will be the same as before. You go off with Gloria, and then you anounce that you're coming back, just like that! Depressed, ha! Who needs you!"

"But, Samantha," answered Bradley in a shocked voice, "didn't you miss me?"

"I did at first, because I was lonely," said Samantha thoughtfully, "but then I realized that it was a lot more pleasent around here without you. You're not easy to live with, you know. You're very damanding. And what about Gloria?"

"Demanding? Me?" asked a surprised Bradley. "I don't know what you mean. As for Gloria, she doesn't understand. When I suggested that she take the baby after you have it, she absulotely rafused. I don't know what's wrong with her. So here I am."

Samantha stood completely still for a moment, and then she said wonderingly, "You're crazy, Bradley. You know, you really are nuts."

Bradley reached out a hand toward her. "But Samantha, what about the baby? Think of him. Doesn't he need both of us as parents? We should stay together for the baby."

"Yes, I've thought of that," answered Samantha quietly, sitting down. "Maybe for the good of the baby, I should take you back. I don't know. I have to think about it some more." She looked at him firmly. "You'll just have to wait until I decide what to do."

"What about what I think?" demanded Bradley. "I *am* the father."

"I spent our entire marriage listening to what you thought and doing only what you wanted. Now it's time for me to think for myself." She stood up and handed him his coat. "When I make my decision, I'll let you know."

Chapter 19

David

David

Part 1

Vocabulary

These are the vocabulary words you will learn in this chapter. Each word has a definition and a sentence. Notice that many words have more than one meaning.

1. **startle** (verb)—to surprise or shock; (adjective)—surprised, shocked
   When the boy jumped up, he startled his mother.
   She was startled when she looked up from her book and saw Chey standing next to her.

2. **mutter** (verb)
   1) to speak in a low, unclear voice
      Please speak loudly and clearly. When you mutter I can't understand you.
   2) to speak in a low angry voice; to complain
      The crowd of people in front of the courthouse began to mutter tensely when the policeman demanded that they all go home.

3. **conversation** (noun)—talk between two or more people
   I assume that Tony and Donald were having a pleasant conversation because they were both smiling.

4. **rough** (adjective)
   1) difficult, unpleasant
      After her mother died, the poor little girl had a rough time.
      The teacher gave us a rough homework assignment.

2) not gentle, tough

Football is a rough sport.

The hurricane brought us rough weather.

3) not smooth

*When Moe tried to fold the stiff, rough wallpaper, he cut his
hands.*

4) unfinished, not exact

*I'm not a good artist. This is just a rough drawing of what our
new house will look like.*

*Please explain. I have only a rough idea of what you're talking
about.*

5. **bagel** (noun) — a hard round roll with a hole in it

*Doughnuts are soft and sweet, but bagels are harder and more like
bread.*

6. **company** (noun)

1) a group of people in business together

He works for the gas company.

2) a group of people together for a purpose

The Boston Ballet is a dance company.

*The captain wanted to make his company into the best one in
the army.*

3) visitors, guests

We're having company for Thanksgiving.

4) people to be with, friendship

*"Marta is in the hospital, and I think she'd like some company.
Let's go see her," Joe suggested.*

7. **stir** (verb)

1) to move

The wind stirred the leaves on the trees.

2) to mix by moving around with a spoon, fork, etc.

Before using it, stir the paint with a stick to mix the colors.

3) to cause

*If you refuse to tell Joyce you're sorry, you will only stir up
more bad feelings.*

8. **cheer**
   1) (verb)—to yell, showing happiness or support; (noun)—a yell of happiness or support
      When they announced that John F. Kennedy would be the new president, everyone began to cheer.
      Three cheers for the captain of our team!
   2) (verb)—to make a sad person happy; (noun)—happiness
      Beautiful music always cheers me when I'm feeling sad.
      Santa Claus brings cheer on Christmas.
      I heard you lost your job so I brought you some flowers to cheer you up.
      The little girl is nuts about cats, so her father bought her a book about cats to cheer her up when she was sick.

9. **warn** (verb)—to tell about something bad that might happen
   I forgot to warn Johnny that the floor was wet, and he fell and hurt his leg.
   Please come in, but I'm warning you, the house is a mess!

10. **worn**
    1) (past participle of *wear*)—put on the body
       Have you worn your new coat yet?
    2) (adjective)—used and old (also, idiom—*worn out*)
       These tires are so worn that we will have to get new ones.
       This old coat is worn out.
    3) *worn out* (idiom)—very tired, exhausted
       After the big football game, the team was completely worn out.

11. **subject** (noun)
    1) something you're talking, thinking, reading, or writing about; (grammar) the person or thing you're talking about in a sentence that does the action
       The subject of tonight's talk is "Collecting Stamps."
       "George" is the subject of the sentence, "George wants to settle in Kansas City."
    2) something you study in school
       I'm studying three subjects: English, math, and history.

12. **figure**
    1) (noun)—a shape, especially of a person
       Juana saw a dark figure outside the window, but she couldn't
       see if it was a person or an animal.
       The sexy actress has a beautiful figure.
    2) (noun)—a famous person
       Susan B. Anthony is an important figure in American history.
    3) (noun)—a number or amount
       "7" and "10" are figures.
       This figure will tell you the total amount of money that you
       have to pay.
    4) (verb)—*figure (it) out* (idiom)—to try to understand or find an an-
       swer to a problem
       Samantha is trying to figure out what to do about her
       pregnancy.
       I've been working on this puzzle for an hour, but I can't figure it
       out.

Idioms

Idioms are words that have special meanings in English when used
together.

1. **do her best**—do something as well as she can
   She did her best to get to her appointment on time, but the bus was
   late.
   I always do my best to make Christmas a special time for everyone.

2. **bring it up**—talk about it
   "I have something important to say, and I thought this would be a
   good time to bring it up," Huong said solemnly.
   It wasn't Ty that suggested the change in the rules; Alicia brought it
   up.

3. **I don't mind**—it doesn't bother me
   I don't mind if you go first.
   She doesn't mind if we stop at the store before we go to the movies.

Part 2

Vocabulary

Complete each of the following sentences with one of the words on the list. Don't forget to read the words before the blank *and* the words after the blank to help you find the missing vocabulary word.

    Remember that all the answers (a, b, c) under one number are different meanings of the same word. When a word has more than one meaning, there is a parenthesis ( ) after the sentence. In the parenthesis put the number of the meaning from the vocabulary list in Part 1.

stir	company
bagel	figure
startle	warn
conversation	worn
rough	mutter
subject	cheer

1. I had a _____ with my friend today, and he told me about

   his trip.

2. a) His favorite _____ in school is math. ( )

   b) What is the _____ of this book? ( )

3. a) When you put sugar in coffee, you usually _____ it with

   a spoon so the sugar doesn't sink to the bottom of the cup and

   stay there. ( )

   b) That boy always comes here to _____ up trouble. ( )

   c) I heard the children _____ in the other room, so I knew

   they were awake. ( )

4. The sudden noise _____ (d) her.

5. a) When the teacher announced the test, the class started to

    _____ . ( )

  b) He _____ (ed) to himself while he worked. ( )

6. a) What _____ did he give you when you asked the price

    of the car? ( )

  b) I saw a tall _____ in the doorway, but I couldn't see

    who it was. ( )

  c) The president is an important public _____. ( )

  d) She tried to _____ out the math problem, but it was too

    hard. ( )

7. a) She cut her finger on the _____ wood. ( )

  b) This is a _____ math problem; I can't figure it out. ( )

  c) Children! Someone will get hurt if you play too

    _____ . ( )

  d) I can't tell you exactly how to do it, but I can give you a

    _____ idea. ( )

8. a) When the batter hit a home run, the crowd began to

    _____ . ( )

  b) People send flowers to the hospital to _____ up the

    patients. ( )

9. a) Martha baked a cake because she is expecting _____

    tomorrow. ( )

  b) The little girl keeps the old man _____. ( )

  c) She works in a big _____. ( )

  d) The soldier's _____ in the army was sent to

    Germany. ( )

10. In New York many people eat a _____ with cream cheese

for breakfast.

11. She _____ (ed) the children not to go in the street.

12. a) She has _____ that sweater every day for a week. ( )

b) My old blanket was so _____ that I had to buy

another. ( )

c) After staying up all night working, he was _____ out. ( )

Idioms

Complete each of the following sentences with one of the idioms on the
list. Don't forget to read the words before the blank *and* the words after
the blank to help you find the missing idioms.

I don't mind
bring it up
do your best

1. I think your idea is absolutely wonderful. Why don't you _____

_____ at our next meeting?

2. We don't expect a perfect job. Just _____ and

that will be good enough.

3. If you don't feel well, we can just stay home and watch TV tonight.

_____ .

Part 3

Summary

Bradley has left Samantha for Gloria. Samantha goes out with John
Paul. When Samantha discovers she is pregnant by her husband Bradley, she tries to decide what to do.

Questions to think and talk about before you read:

- What kind of friend has John Paul been to Samantha?
- What kind of friend has David been to Samantha?

Episode 19. David

The next night, Samantha went out to dinner with John Paul. She did her best to make conversation with him, but her thoughts distracted her. Finally, as they were eating dessert, she said, "I'm sorry, John Paul, I just can't concentrate. I keep thinking about how this decision I'm making is going to affect my whole life."

"Oh, come on," said John Paul. "Forget about it for a while. It's all you talk about. Life goes on, you know."

Samantha looked startled. "This is the first time I've brought it up all evening."

John Paul looked impatient. "Can we change the subject?" he asked.

Samantha picked up her spoon to stir her coffee, and then she said quietly, "I don't want to change the subject. I need to think about it and talk about it until I figure it out. What I don't need is you, John Paul. You don't really care about me at all; all you care about is yourself. I don't want to see you anymore." She got up and put on her coat. "Goodbye, John Paul."

Just as Samantha had arrived home, the doorbell rang. "Now what?" she muttered to herself as she went to the door.

"Hi!" said David. "Are you busy? I just thought I'd drop by and see how you're doing."

Samantha smiled. 'Well, this is a pleasant surprise. Come in!"

"Here," said David, handing her a bag, "I brought you some bagels. I know this is a rough time for you, so I came to cheer you up."

Samantha stood very still with the bagels in her hand and stared at him.

"What's the matter?" he asked, concerned.

"Oh, I'm sorry," she said with tears in her eyes. "It was just so nice of you to think of me, especially after what happened with John Paul earlier this evening. Come on in and have some coffee. I guess I have to warn you, though, I'm not very good company right now. I'm worn out."

"That's okay," answered David as he walked after her into the kitchen. "I don't mind. Maybe talking to me about it will help."

Part 4

Questions

1. Why can't Samantha concentrate during dinner?
2. Does John Paul want to talk to Samantha about what's bothering her? What are two of the things he says that show you that?
3. What does Samantha tell John Paul before she puts on her coat? Why?
4. When Samantha gets home, who comes to the door?
5. Why does he come to visit?
6. What did David do that made Samantha get tears in her eyes?
7. Why does she say that she's not good company?
8. What does David say when Samantha says that she's not good company?
9. How is what David says to Samantha different from what John Paul says to Samantha?
10. Who is a better friend to Samantha, John Paul or David? Why?

Part 5

Use your vocabulary words to complete this crossword puzzle.

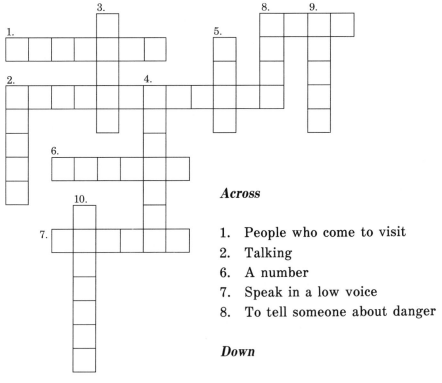

Across

1. People who come to visit
2. Talking
6. A number
7. Speak in a low voice
8. To tell someone about danger

Down

2. To make happy
3. Bread with a hole in it
4. To surprise
5. To move
8. Used and old
9. Difficult
10. What you're talking about

Part 6

There are nine vocabulary words spelled incorrectly in this copy of the story. Find the mistakes and correct them. The first one has been done for you.

The next night, Samantha went out to dinner with John Paul. She
did her best to make ~~conversasion~~ conversation with him, but her thoughts distracted
her. Finally, as they were eating dessert, she said, "I'm sorry, John Paul,
I just can't concentrate. I keep thinking about how this decision I'm
making is going to affect my whole life."

"Oh, come on," said John Paul. "Forget about it for a while. It's all
you talk about. Life goes on, you know."

Samantha looked starteled. "This is the first time I've brought it
up all evening."

John Paul looked impatient. "Can we change the subjict?" he
asked.

Samantha picked up her spoon to stir her coffee, and then she
said quietly, "I don't want to change the subject. I need to think about it
and talk about it until I figer it out. What I don't need is you, John
Paul. You don't really care about me at all; all you care about is yourself. I don't want to see you anymore." She got up and put on her coat.
"Goodbye, John Paul."

Just as Samantha had arrived home, the doorbell rang. "Now
what?" she mutered to herself as she went to the door.

"Hi!" said David. "Are you busy? I just thought I'd drop by and
see how you're doing."

Samantha smiled. 'Well, this is a pleasant surprise. Come in!"

"Here," said David, handing her a bag, "I brought you some
bagels. I know this is a rugh time for you, so I came to chear you up."

Samantha stood very still with the bagels in her hand and stared
at him.

"What's the matter?" he asked, concerned.

"Oh, I'm sorry," she said with tears in her eyes. "It was just so nice of you to think of me, especially after what happened with John Paul earlier this evening. Come on in and have some coffee. I guess I have to worn you, though, I'm not very good company right now. I'm warn out."

"That's okay," answered David as he walked after her into the kitchen. "I don't mind. Maybe talking to me about it will help."

Chapter 20

Samantha Decides

Chapter **20**

Samantha Decides

Part 1

Vocabulary

These are the vocabulary words you will learn in this chapter. Each word has a definition and a sentence. Notice that many words have more than one meaning.

1. **imagine** (verb)—to form a picture in the mind of something not true or present at that moment
   In his song, John Lennon asks us to try and imagine a world of peace.

2. **shout** (verb)—to yell, to call out loudly; (noun)—a yell; a loud call
   Jess startled Natalie when he shouted to warn her that a car was coming.
   There was a loud shout as everyone saw that Ra-shaan was the first runner to finish the race.

3. **spend** (verb)
   1) to use or pass time
      Tom wants to spend his vacation in Italy.
   2) to pay
      Irena spent a lot of money on food that day because she was expecting company.

4. **argument** (noun)—discussion by people who do not agree, a fight in words
   They had an argument over who was the best person to be president.
   The subject of abortion causes a lot of arguments.

5. **lift**
    1) (verb)—to raise, pick up
       Lift the picture over your head so everyone can see it.
       The sound of singing made Wila lift her eyes from the book.
       Her father's visit lifted her spirits when she was in the hospital.
    2) (noun)—a ride
       Somithea gave Jayne a lift to school.

6. **shrug** (verb)—to raise the shoulders to show you don't know or don't care; (noun)—a raise of the shoulders to show you don't know or you don't care
    When we asked him how to get to City Hall, he shrugged and muttered, "How would I know? I'm a stranger here myself."
    When Susan asked him which movie he wanted to see, he gave a shrug and said, "I don't care. Whatever you like."

7. **incredible** (adjective)—hard to believe, seeming to be impossible; **incredibly** (adverb)—in a way that is hard to believe
    It was incredible that Margarita ran into Luis at the bagel shop accidently, after not having seem him for 30 years.
    It is incredibly difficult for two people who don't speak the same language to have a conversation.

8. **birth** (noun)
    1) a baby being born, coming into life; **to give birth**—to have a baby
       Everyone cheered when they heard about the birth of the baby.
       She never imagined she would give birth to twins.
    2) the beginning of something; **to give birth**—to begin something
       The Wright brothers' first airplane ride was the birth of air travel in the United States.
       The end of communism in the Soviet Union gave birth to incredible changes in Europe.

9. **incompatible** (adjective)—not able to live or work together happily; not agreeable
    Patty and Elena had a rough time when they lived together because they are so incompatible.

10. **instant**

    1) (noun)—a short space of time

       I saw the figure in the window for just an instant, and then it was gone.

    2) (noun)—a specific moment in time

       Come here this instant.

       He heard the doorbell at the same instant that the phone rang.

    3) (adjective)—quick; able to be made quickly

       This medicine will give you instant relief.

       To make instant oatmeal, just pour in boiling water and stir.

11. **stretch**

    1) (verb)—to make something larger or longer by pulling on it

       Rubber can stretch.

       This sheet is a little small, so you need to stretch it to get it to fit over the corner.

    2) (verb)—to reach out as long as possible, to extend; (noun)—a long reach

       She had to stretch out her arm to close the window on the other side of the car.

       When he woke up in the morning he gave his arms and legs a big stretch.

    3) (verb)—to extend from one place to another, to go the length of; (noun)—a length

       The mountains stretched for miles.

       I hope my paycheck will stretch until next payday.

       Be careful. There's a bad stretch of road ahead.

       Sheila has had a stretch of bad luck.

12. **control**

    1) (verb)—to direct, to have power over; (noun)—power, direction

       Those two policemen control the traffic on this stretch of road.

       When his car hit the ice, Dean lost control of the car.

    2) (verb)—to hold back, resist; (noun)—a holding back

       Even though he knew she loved someone else, he couldn't control his feelings for her.

       Children, don't run around like that. Control yourselves.

       During my argument with Cheryl, I lost control and started to shout.

3) **controls** (noun)—parts used for directing a machine
   The controls on this machine are complicated; can you teach me how to use them?

Idioms

1. **on her own**—alone, depending only on herself
   You can't help her with this. She has to do it on her own.
   I did it all on my own.

2. **help out**—to help
   Sally's moving, so I stopped by to see if I could help out.
   I can't lift this by myself. Can you help me out?

3. **fall in love**—to love, begin to love
   I'm afraid to fall in love with you.
   He fell in love with her the first time he saw her.

4. **grow up**—grow from a child to an adult
   I grew up in the country, but my children will grow up in the city.

5. **go along**—continue, go forward
   Let's sing as we go along.

6. **get out**—leave
   Call me the instant you get out of the meeting.

Part 2

Vocabulary

Complete each of the following sentences with one of the words on the list. Don't forget to read the words before the blank *and* the words after the blank to help you find the missing vocabulary word.

Remember that all the answers (a, b, c) under one number are different meanings of the same word. When a word has more than one meaning, there is a parenthesis ( ) after the sentence. In the parenthesis put the number of the meaning from the vocabulary list in Part 1.

imagine   incredible
control   lift
incompatible birth
shrug   shout
spend   argument
stretch   instant

1. a) At Christmas time everyone has to _____ a lot of money. ( )

   b) Betty likes to _____ time with her grandchildren. ( )

2. a) She looked up, and at that _____ she saw the two cars crash. ( )

   b) Coffee lovers usually don't like _____ coffee. ( )

   c) Closing your eyes only takes an _____. ( )

3. They thought his story about people from other worlds was

   _____.

4. a) The baby weighed 7 pounds at _____. ( )

   b) On July 4, Americans celebrate the _____ of the United States. ( )

5. a) He was so upset that he couldn't _____ his feelings. ( )

   b) The general took _____ of the army. ( )

   c) The pilot operates the _____ (s) of the airplane. ( )

6. They got divorced because they were _____.

7. a) Don't _____ the elastic too far or it will break. ( )

   b) You should _____ before you exercise. ( )

   c) The whole ocean _____ (ed) out before us. ( )

8. The poor woman tried to _____ what it would be like to be rich.

9. When the teacher asked her a question she _____ (ged) her

   shoulders because she didn't know the answer.

10. There was a lot of noise because everyone was _____ (ing).

11. a) This suitcase is too heavy to _____. ( )

    b) Her friend had a car, so she asked for a _____ to the

       store. ( )

12. Elizabeth and her husband had an _____ over whose turn it

    was to wash the dishes.

Idioms

Complete each of the following sentences with one of the idioms on the
list. Don't forget to read the words before the blank *and* the words after
the blank to help you find the missing idioms.

get out	go along
help out	grow up
on his own	fall in love

1. Joan is worn out with working and taking care of two sick children.

   She needs someone to _____.

2. Everyone could see that John and Yoko were beginning to

   _____.

3. If we don't _____ of the house by 2:00, we'll

   be late for the movie.

4. After his wife died, Tony had to learn to take care of his son

   _____.

5. "I want to be a baseball player when I _____,"

   said the little boy.

6. I don't know where it is, but let's go. You can give me directions as

we _____ .

Part 3

Summary

After Bradley leaves Samantha for Gloria, Samantha goes out with
John Paul. When Samantha discovers she is pregnant by her husband
Bradley, she tries to decide what to do.

Questions to think and talk about before you read:

- What do you think about Samantha's relationship with David?
- What do you think will be Samantha's final decision?

Episode 20. Samantha Decides

It was Sunday. Samantha had decided to spend the day alone,
thinking, but the telephone just wouldn't stop ringing.

When Bradley called to see if she'd made a decision, she said no.
When David called to see if she wanted to go out to dinner, she said
yes. When Jasmine called to see if she was all right, she said she was
fine.

"I've got to get out of here so that I can think," she thought to
herself. "Time for another walk on the beach!"

When she got to the beach there were very few people around,
and she walked on the sand and looked at the ocean.

"Do I want this baby or not?" she asked herself. She thought
about her little niece. She thought about the kids in her neighborhood.
She thought about how she'd always planned to have a child. She imagined herself with a baby; giving birth to it, nursing it, playing with it.
In that instant she knew that she did want the baby.

But then she thought about Bradley. She thought about the arguments they'd had, and how demanding he was to live with. She thought
about how much happier she'd been this last month, being on her own,

in control of her own life, and she knew it would be incredibly difficult for her to live with him again, even for the good of the baby.

"How good is it for a child, anyway, to grow up with parents who dislike each other, who are totally incompatible?" she thought. "But that would mean I'd have to raise the baby on my own. Could I do it alone? Am I strong enough?"

She stopped and looked out at the ocean stretched out before her. "Why not?" she thought with growing excitement. "I don't have to depend on Bradley or John Paul. I can depend on myself! I'll learn as I go along. One nice thing about Bradley is that he wants to be a father. He would help out. Jasmine would help too, and so would David."

She thought about David. They had been seeing a lot of each other the last few days. What was going to happen with that? It would be nice to have a relationship that had been a friendship first. He was so kind to her, so caring.

She shrugged. She couldn't worry about that now. If she and David fell in love, that would be wonderful, but she couldn't depend on it. She had to take care of herself and her baby now.

She lifted up her arms to the sky and the ocean. "I can do it!" she shouted to the sun and the waves. "I can do it alone!"

Part 4

Questions

1. Why did Samantha go to the beach?
2. What does she think about on the beach?
3. Does she decide that she wants the baby, or not?
4. Does she want to go back with Bradley? Why or why not?
5. How does she feel about having the baby alone?
6. Who is the most important person she can depend on?
7. Who does she think would help her?
8. What has been happening between Samantha and David?
9. What is more important to her right now, her relationship with David or the baby?
10. What does Samantha decide to do in the end?
11. What do you think of her decision? Do you think it was a good one or not?

Part 5

Put the correct vocabulary word in each blank in the story. Use the words *before* and *after* the blank to help you find the correct vocabulary word.

imagine	incredible
control	lift
incompatible	birth
shrug	shout
spend	argument
stretch	instant

My husband and I were so _____ that we finally broke up. We had too many _____ (s) and fights that we just couldn't _____ .

Now, alone with the kids and the house, and working all day, I don't have enough time to _____ on anything! I wake up and _____ and then I don't stop running until the _____ I fall into bed at night. I'm so tired it's _____ , but what can I do? I _____ and I go on and try not to _____ at the kids.

But when I remember the _____ of my baby or _____ the older one out of his bed, I know my children mean everything to me. I can't _____ living my life any other way.

Part 6

There are eight vocabulary words spelled incorrectly in this copy of the story. Find the mistakes and correct them. The first one has been done for you.

It was Sunday. Samantha had decided to spend the day alone, thinking, but the telephone just wouldn't stop ringing.

When Bradley called to see if she'd made a decision, she said no. When David called to see if she wanted to go out to dinner, she said yes. When Jasmine called to see if she was all right, she said she was fine.

"I've got to get out of here so that I can think," she thought to herself. "Time for another walk on the beach!"

When she got to the beach there were very few people around, and she walked on the sand and looked at the ocean.

"Do I want this baby or not?" she asked herself. She thought about her little niece. She thought about the kids in her neighborhood. She thought about how she'd always planned to have a child. She ~~imagined~~ imagined herself with a baby; giving berth to it, nursing it, playing with it. In that instent she knew that she did want the baby.

But then she thought about Bradley. She thought about the arguments they'd had, and how demanding he was to live with. She thought about how much happier she'd been this last month, being on her own, in cuntrol of her own life, and she knew it would be incredably difficult for her to live with him again, even for the good of the baby.

"How good is it for a child, anyway, to grow up with parents who dislike each other, who are totally incompatable?" she thought. "But that would mean I'd have to raise the baby on my own. Could I do it alone? Am I strong enough?"

She stopped and looked out at the ocean streched out before her. "Why not?" she thought with growing excitement. "I don't have to depend on Bradley or John Paul. I can depend on myself! I'll learn as I

293 / Chapter 20

go along. One nice thing about Bradley is that he wants to be a father. He would help out. Jasmine would help too, and so would David."

She thought about David. They had been seeing a lot of each other the last few days. What was going to happen with that? It would be nice to have a relationship that had been a friendship first. He was so kind to her, so caring.

She shrugged. She couldn't worry about that now. If she and David fell in love, that would be wonderful, but she couldn't depend on it. She had to take care of herself and her baby now.

She lifted up her arms to the sky and the ocean. "I can do it!" she showted to the sun and the waves. "I can do it alone!"

After the Decision

After the Decision

Part 1

Being a Single Parent

Questions to think and talk about before you read:

- What is a single parent? What is life like for a single parent?

After the birth of Samantha's baby, Samantha will be a single parent, a parent who raises a child by herself or himself. There have always been people who became single parents because of the death of a husband or wife, or sometimes the break-up of a marriage, but in general single parents were unusual. Now one-parent families are becoming much more common.

One reason is that there are so many more divorces than ever before. Another is that more women who get pregnant when they are not married are keeping their babies and raising them alone. The United States Census Bureau, the government department that counts and gets information on the American people, says that in 1960 9% (9 people out of 100) of American families were single-parent families. In 1970 the number was 12%, and in 1986 the number of single-parent families went up to 24%. Although there are more single fathers who live with their children than before, most of these single parents are women. When a family breaks up or a pregnant woman is not married, the children usually stay with the mother.

It's not easy being a single parent. One person must do all of the work both in and out of the home that two people do in a two-parent family. The single parent, usually the mother, must do all the care for the children and all the housework, as well as bring money into the house to support the family. There is a lot of *stress*, or pressure, on a single parent.

One *stress*, or difficulty, on the single mother is how to bring enough money, or *income*, into the family. The father usually makes more money than the mother, if she works, and when the marriage breaks up and he leaves, the mother and children are almost always poorer than before. They must live on the money she makes. If she is not working, she must go out and get a job, and often she does not have the education or work experience to find one. She may feel uncomfortable leaving small children with another person while she works, or be unable to find a person to take care of them. It is often difficult to find a good day-care center or babysitter, or the day care may be too expensive for her to afford on her work *income*, or money. Many single mothers are forced to get government help through the AFDC (Aid to Families with Dependent Children) program in order to support their children.

The father should pay the single mother child support, a weekly payment of money to help support the children, and this is usually ordered by the courts. *Receiving*, or getting, child support can be a help to the single-parent family, but many fathers refuse to pay it, and the mother must support the family on her own.

Another *stress* for the single parent is *conflict*, or problems and fighting, in the family. The children may feel angry or depressed because their father does not live with them and they don't see him very much. They may show this by being angry at one or both parents, but it is most often the single mother they live with who must try to help them with this. The separated parents may be angry at each other, because of *conflicts*, or problems, they had when they were together. This may confuse or upset the children, and they may feel forced to take the side of one parent or the other. It will help the children if the parents try not to involve the children in the parents' *conflicts*.

The support of family and friends can make the single parent's job easier. Friends and family members can do household jobs, babysit for the children, and give the single mother emotional support. They can help her make a good life for herself and her children.

There can be some *benefits*, or good things, about living in a one-parent family. In a single-parent family, the parent and children may spend more time together than they do in a two-parent family. Because they don't have another adult at home to do some of the work, they must depend on each other, and work together. This can cause the children and the single parent to have a very special, close relationship.

Because they help out more at home, the children often learn to do things on their own at an earlier age. They become more *independent;* they are able to think and act for themselves. The single mother also may become more *independent.* She learns to depend on herself and control her own life.

Both single parents and children also have the *benefit* of living in a calmer, happier home than they would be in a family where the parents stay together, but are always fighting. As Samantha says, "How good is it ... for a child to grow up with parents who dislike each other, who are totally incompatible?" A home without the constant daily *conflict* and tension of fighting parents may be better for everyone.

Finally, a single parent and her children can be as loving, caring, happy, and strong as any other parents and children in any other family. Although life may not always be easy for the one-parent family, single-parent families, like other families, can be healthy, happy places for adults and children to live in and grow.

Part 2

Questions

1. What is a single parent?
2. Name two ways a person becomes a single parent.
3. Are there more, or fewer, single parents today than before?
4. Name three reasons a single parent often has trouble bringing money into the family.
5. Name one conflict in the single-parent family.
6. Who can make the single parent's job easier?
7. Name one benefit of living in a single-parent family.

Part 3

Vocabulary

There are a few new words in what you have just read. You should be able to understand the meanings of these words by reading the words *before* and *after* them.

Fill in the blanks with the words that go with the definitions. If you're not sure of the meanings of the words, look back at the story. Usually the definition of the word is in the same sentence as the word.

stress   conflict
income   benefits
receiving   independent

1. money coming into a family   _____
2. good things   _____
3. problems, fighting   _____
4. getting   _____
5. pressure, difficulty   _____
6. able to depend on yourself   _____

Part 4

Vocabulary Review

This is a review of all the vocabulary words you have learned in Chapters 16-20. Match each word on the left with the definition on the right by putting the correct letter in the blank. Look back at the words in the chapters if you need help with any of the definitions.

Chapters 16–18

A.

1. impatient	_____	a. to turn over and over
2. silence	_____	b. ask for something in a restaurant
3. abandon	_____	c. bringing relief, calm
4. firm	_____	d. say no
5. reach	_____	e. sudden, done from your feelings
6. order	_____	f. pick up, lift
7. soothing	_____	g. strong, not easily moved
8. refuse	_____	h. tell in a formal way

9. impulsive　　_____　　i.　complete quiet

10. sink　　_____　　j.　leave, give up

11. roll　　_____　　k.　yell

12. announce　　_____　　l.　able to touch

13. scream　　_____　　m.　go down in water

14. assume　　_____　　n.　believe to be true
without being told

15. raise　　_____　　o.　not willing to wait

B.

1. groan　　_____　　a.　the part of something
you hold

2. hysterical　　_____　　b.　wanting very much

3. pleasant　　_____　　c.　serious

4. solution　　_____　　d.　divide, go different
ways

5. irritate　　_____　　e.　nice

6. solemn　　_____　　f.　very funny

7. breathe　　_____　　g.　bother

8. breath　　_____　　h.　to bend part of something over another part

9. handle　　_____　　i.　a sound made in pain

10. separate　　_____　　j.　fight against

11. absolutely　　_____　　k.　the air you take in

12. fold　　_____　　l.　so good it cannot be
made better

13. perfect　　_____　　m.　completely

14. eager　　_____　　n.　to take air in and out

15. resist　　_____　　o.　answer to a problem

Chapters 18-20

A.

1. company　　_____　　a.　mix

2. figure　　_____　　b.　a roll with a hole in it

3. tense　　_____　　c.　yell

4. lift　　_____　　d.　visitors

5. bagel　　_____　　e.　a fight in words

6. shout	_____	f.	nervous
7. incredible	_____	g.	pay
8. suggest	_____	h.	talk
9. control	_____	i.	not smooth
10. settle	_____	j.	pick up, raise
11. stir	_____	k.	to offer an idea
12. argument	_____	l.	hard to believe
13. conversation	_____	m.	to go live in a place
14. rough	_____	n.	a shape
15. spend	_____	o.	to direct, have power over

B.

1. cheer	_____	a.	to surprise
2. subject	_____	b.	to think of something not true at that moment
3. nut	_____	c.	to speak in a low, unclear voice
4. birth	_____	d.	something you're talking about
5. startle	_____	e.	a short space of time
6. stretch	_____	f.	to yell, showing happiness
7. mutter	_____	g.	a baby coming into life
8. shrug	_____	h.	person who does crazy things
9. demand	_____	i.	to tell about something bad about to happen
10. instant	_____	j.	not able to live together happily
11. collect	_____	k.	ask for strongly
12. incompatible	_____	l.	to raise the shoulders to show you don't know
13. warn	_____	m.	to group together
14. worn	_____	n.	to make longer by pulling
15. imagine	_____	o.	used and old

Part 5

Idioms Review

This is a review of all the idioms you have learned in Chapters 16-20.
Match the part of the sentence on the left that goes together with the
end of the sentence on the right by putting the correct letter in the
blank.

Chapters 16–18

1. When he saw the
   incredible sight, his
   mouth . . .   _____

2. After their big fight,
   Max and Lisa could
   never get . . .   _____

3. When he asked her to
   marry him she hugged
   him and jumped up
   and down. She's
   happy all . . .   _____

4. He shrugged and said,
   "I don't know where
   Uncle Harry is. He
   likes to go . . .   _____

5. "I don't want to see
   you or talk to you,"
   he said as he
   turned . . .   _____

6. First I can't find my
   glasses, and now I've
   lost my keys. Oh . . .   _____

7. These pants will
   never stretch enough
   to fit you. The
   thing . . .   _____

8. If she doesn't have a
   good reason for being
   late she makes . . .   _____

a. right.
b. it up.
c. here a lot
   lately.
d. fell open.
e. back together
   again.
f. to the point.
g. about her?
h. off by himself.

9. I don't ever want to
see you again—the
hell...
10. You talk too much.
Get... _____
11. Randy has been
around... _____
12. You gave everyone a
Christmas present
except Beth. What... _____

i. his back.
j. brother.
k. is, they're just
too small.
l. with you.

Chapters 18-20

1. Amanda has been cry-
ing all day. What's... _____
2. Don't try to help her.
She likes to do things
on... _____
3. George and I disliked
each other at... _____
4. There's a lot to do in
the kitchen. Can you
help... _____
5. I try to do my... _____
6. If you think there's a
fire, get... _____
7. He suddenly got up
and left the restau-
rant, just... _____
8. Come with me to the
store. You can tell me
about your trip as we
go... _____
9. I have a problem to
discuss with you. Is
this a good time to
bring... _____

a. up so fast.
b. like that, and I
had to pay the
check for both
of us.
c. along.
d. wrong with
her?
e. don't mind.
f. best at every-
thing I try.
g. in love?
h. first, but now
we're good
friends.
i. out by washing
the dishes?

10. I'll do the shopping
    for you. I . . .   _____   j. her own.
                                                        k. it up?
11. Children seem to   l. out of the
    grow . . .   _____   house
                                                           immediately.
12. Do you think David
    and Samantha will
    fall . . .   _____

Index of Vocabulary Words and Idioms

The number indicates the chapter where the word or idiom is introduced.

Vocabulary Words

warn, 19
waste, 6
wave, 5
wealthy, 5
wipe, 13
withdraw, 3
wonder, 4
worn, 19

Idioms

after all, 1
all right, 17
a lot, 2
around here, 18
as long as, 14
as soon as, 2
as soon as possible, 7
at first, 18
at least, 6

break someone's heart, 1
bring it up, 19

catch herself, 4
come by, 5
come over, 13

did her best, 19
drive someone crazy, 12

each other, 15
even if, 14
ever since, 11

fall asleep, 14
fall in love, 20
fix things up, 6

get a hold of yourself, 3
get away with, 3
get back together, 16
get out, 20
get rid of, 15
get to know, 8
get to the point, 16
get up, 12
give someone a checkup, 12

give the child up, 13
give up, 7
go along, 20
go back, 13
go off, 18
go on, 13
go out with, 10
grow up, 20

have nothing to do with me, 14
head in his hands, 9
help out, 20
hold back, 8
how sweet, 5

I'd love to, 4
I don't mind, 19
if only, 1

just like that, 18

life savings, 5
lips met hers, 8
little while, 8
looking into her eyes, 4
look up to, 1

make it up, 17
make up, 7
mouth fell open, 16

never mind, 11
no matter what, 14
none of his business, 15

of course, 14
oh brother, 16
oh my goodness, 2
oh no, 12
on his own, 20

pay attention to, 6
point of view, Review 11-15

run into, 9
run out on, 11

say so, 10
see, 10